# Real Faith in the Real God in the Real World

## Joyce Schramm

*Joyce Schramm*

*Nehemiah 8:10*

TRILOGY CHRISTIAN PUBLISHERS

*TUSTIN, CA*

Trilogy Christian Publishers
A Wholly Owned Subsidiary of Trinity Broadcasting Network
2442 Michelle Drive
Tustin, CA 92780

For information, address Trilogy Christian Publishing

Rights Department, 2442 Michelle Drive, Tustin, Ca 92780.

Trilogy Christian Publishing/ TBN and colophon are trademarks of Trinity Broadcasting Network.

For information about special discounts for bulk purchases, please contact Trilogy Christian Publishing.

Cover Photo: Jude Beck

Manufactured in the United States of America

10 9 8 7 6 5 4 3 2 1

Library of Congress Cataloging-in-Publication Data is available.

ISBN 978-1-64773-672-9

ISBN 978-1-64773-673-6 (ebook)

# Contents

# Endorsements

Thoughtful, tender, provoking, a current that carries you more deeply into your walk with Jesus by joining Joyce on her journey. It is a privilege to be allowed to travel with her and our Lord.

**Angie Zagorski**
Speech Language Pathologist

I identified with Joyce's challenges and struggles. Her sharing helped me to access the Presence of God and receive hope and comfort. I read her story through tears of gratitude.

**Evelyn McDonald**
Elementary Teacher, retired

A sweet, sensitive, and instructional book! Joyce Schramm opens the curtain into her life and lets the reader gather encouraging and instructional examples for growing deeper in one's relationship with the Lord. As a pastor's spouse, I could identify with many of her challenges. Her sweetness and love of the Lord shine through. Her wit, intelligence, and willingness to listen and learn will instruct many to persist in their quest to experience *Real Faith in the Real God in the Real World*.

**Paula Gast**

Pastor's Wife, Pastoral Counselor, & Retreat Leader


Joyce's descriptive sharing of her intimate relationship with our Lord greatly inspired and encouraged me. Mixing humor with the "mighty miracles of His works to perform" makes *Real Faith in the Real God in the Real World* a good read.

**Susan Zimmerman**

Former Area Board, Women's Aglow Fellowship, Former Charisma Sales Manager for 4 Magazine Card Packs, Sales Manager for Cornerstone Christian Magazine, Director of Caring Ministries

Joyce's style is a joy! Her thoughts woven with the events that first evoked them give an immediacy to the writing. She collars the reader. Each one of them is on the front row.

**Jeanne Strother**
English Instructor, Ball State University

In this delightful book, Joyce Schramm delivers on the promise of the key word in her title, "REAL." The work that she has created here is utterly REAL— unbendingly truthful and unflinchingly honest. Yet, amazingly, this real story is woven into a style that is gentle, humble, and resounding with God's love and grace. Joyce not only seeks to tell you a story, she invites you to take a journey with her, and in the end it is a journey well worth the taking. The story she weaves is as real, gracious, and authentic as the lady I have been privileged to know for most of my life, and through her God has given a gift to the hearts of those seeking to know Him in a deeper, yet much more REAL way.

**Mark Wilkins**
Pastor and Author

"Pastor's wife, mother of four" is a job description with high expectations—and often haunted by crippling self-doubt. Joyce Schramm overcame these challenges and mended relationships by relentlessly pursuing God. A consummate storyteller, Schramm shares insights from more than sixty years in ministry and seventy years of living for the real God in the real world.

John Paff
Principal at Petra Strategic Communication, LLC,
and Editor of *ChristianCollegeDaily.com*.

# Dedication

To my godly mother, Sarah Stafford Arnold, who lived a life of genuine, overcoming faith.

# Acknowledgements

I owe a great debt to my dear husband, David, who encouraged me to write my story and supported me faithfully.

Thank you, Mary Jane Bogle, my sweet daughter. Your editing and computer skills have been invaluable to me. Without your help my story would probably have stayed in a journal buried in a box in the attic.

Many thanks to my prayer partners for your intercession on my behalf.

Above all, I owe everything to the Lord, who called me to write and inspired my thoughts as they flowed through His inspiration.

# Introduction

"Mommy, is Santa Claus real? How can he travel all around the world in just one night?" Our parents could keep the fantasy going only so long. The truth inevitably came out. It was Mommy or Daddy who bought the presents and ate the cookies. As children, we were fooled. Santa Claus was not omnipresent, although he seemed to show up on every street corner. Neither was he omniscient. He really wasn't watching to see if we were naughty or nice.

But the grownups in our lives also told us that there is Someone who is all-knowing and all-powerful and ever-present. He is our heavenly Father that we can't see. But He is still there, just like Santa Claus. As children we wanted to believe, but the seeds of doubt had been planted. Unfortunately, those seeds have a pesky way of surfacing—especially in difficulties.

When we lose our job or a loved one, we wonder if He sees or if He cares. Is He even there? Fears plague us that maybe we've been too naughty for Him to come to our house, and so we quit trying to talk to Him. We drift into indifference and disillusionment. Eventually we put His book on the shelf alongside *'Twas The Night Before Christmas* and turn our backs on another beautiful story. But sometimes we long for a loving father who gives good gifts and comforts us in the dark.

Like most children growing up in American in the 1950s, darkness and doubt did not threaten me in my childhood. That came later. Living in a rural Christian community, surrounded by loving family, friends, and a supportive church fellowship, I felt secure and confident that God was in His heaven and all was right with the world. We didn't lock our doors, and children were free to roam and explore. Honesty and the Golden Rule were the norm.

Nurtured in this environment, I surrendered my life to God at an early age, embracing Biblical truth and endeavoring to live by that truth. For me, Christianity was more about a relationship with a loving Father than a list of rules to follow. His inner voice gave me direction and became a light to guide me. That voice was loud and clear, causing me to know that He was alive and real and that He knew and cared about me and my future.

But in college, shadows of doubt threatened the Light within, nearly blocking it out. During a family crisis, God made Himself known once more, but my preoccupation with my own agenda overshadowed my communication with Him, leaving me vulnerable to doubt again.

As a young mom and pastor's wife, life brought stresses that forced me to face my doubts and admit that my faith was insufficient to help me cope with life. Striving to be a good homemaker, mother of three babies in three years, and the perfect pastor's wife began to take a heavy toll. Added to these pressures was my growing disillusionment with the Church in modern times. Frustration and fatigue opened the door to a growing sense of depression.

But God did not abandon me. Through many ups and downs I found a real faith that did not waver in the real God who intervened in the struggles of my everyday, real life. Above all I found a lasting relationship with my Father, who still gives me good gifts and comforts me in the dark—so much better than Santa Claus.

If you struggle as I have struggled, I pray that my story will encourage you to listen for God's voice and let Him lead you out of the confusion, hopelessness, and doubt that permeate our society. He is a loving father who wants only the best for his children. He says, "I have loved you with an everlasting love; I have drawn you with loving-kindness" (Jeremiah 31:3, NIV). My desire is that you would join me as I dialogue with my Father, my Savior, and my Counselor and find for yourself a real faith in the real God in the real world.

# CHAPTER 1

# Early Faith

Jesus, You are the lover of my soul. Early in life you awakened my desire for You. In the open expanse of Indiana farmland, the heavens declared your glory. On a hilltop, surrounded by Your expansive horizon, I worshipped You under the dome of Your natural cathedral. Tantalizingly close, yet so far away, You wooed me, awakening a deep longing for You. In the grandest courtship ritual in all creation, You displayed Your majesty and beauty, capturing my imagination and my heart. I reached for You but could not touch You.

Then You reached down and touched me. At the altar of my little country church, I felt Your presence, I heard Your call, and I gave you my heart. Although I was very young, I knew something marvelous had happened. On my walk home from church, I felt clean and new. More importantly, I felt very close to You. You were no longer out there beyond the stars where I could not reach You.

Your presence seemed to permeate all of life around me.

Living on the farm, I observed Your love and trustworthiness in the orderliness of the changing seasons; the beauty of trees, flowers, and rivers that renewed us, and Your provision in the seed and harvest. Even in times of disaster, I saw Your rescue and support through the generosity of Your people.

I knew from the Bible that we live in a fallen world where problems exist, but from its pages I learned Your answers to those problems. The stories I read were accounts of people who messed up big time, but through Your forgiveness and presence they overcame giant obstacles to become great leaders and teachers.

Later, I realized more fully that the Bible is raw and real, full of tragedy and triumph. But as a child, I thrilled to the adventures and memorized truths that would rescue and sustain me in adulthood. As a teenager, I continued to follow Your way, but my commitment to school and many activities began to dominate my time, infringing on my time with You. As a result, church attendance and Bible Study became more perfunctory. I still lived by the Bible rules, but You knew that my relationship with You was cooling. You also knew that without relationship, rules alone can lead to legalism and empty pride.

Yet You did not turn Your back on me. You spoke and called me into renewed relationship with You. While sitting in the back pew filled with whispering teenagers, You invaded the space around me. The air was electrified and heavy with Your presence. You spoke in a voice so loud and clear that I was sure the whole church could hear it: "At the close of this service, you will go forward and dedicate your life completely to me."

*Not now, Lord,* I thought. *What will my friends think? What will the pastor think? We don't have altar calls in our church anymore. I'll speak to the pastor after the service. Better yet, I'll go to his home this week, but not now.*

You silenced each argument by repeating the same command. At the end of the service, I responded to Your magnetic pull and walked to the altar, obeying Your voice. I knew You were real. I knew You had spoken to me. I knew You had claimed me for life.

This claim became startlingly real when You intervened in my choice for a life partner. I had been dating a very nice young man who had felt the call to ministry. I was sure You had brought us together, but one day You totally surprised me. Sitting across the room from him, I heard You say, "He will not be the father of your children."

I was stunned and disbelieving. This was a message I did not want to receive. Everything seemed so right about this relationship. Stubbornly, I convinced myself that the thought that had come was only some hesitation in myself.

But the more I tried to hold onto my dreams, the more the relationship began to fall apart. Only later did I realize that You had better plans for each of us and had put up a roadblock to keep us both from missing Your best. In time, You healed my heart and gave me Your song to sing as I went on with life.

During my college years, however, doubt and confusion began to rob me of Your song as I began to listen to the world's lyrics. Subtly I began to sing a different tune. O, Lord, forgive me for the times I have sung my own song, done my own thing. As the Hebrew children, I took the reins of my life and often wandered in futility.

In those college years, I set aside Your counsel and followed after the "enlightened" words of mere men. History professors challenged me to examine my simplistic faith, comparing Christianity with the myriad of world religions. Why should I think that Christianity embodied the truth? Didn't I realize that Christianity is not unique, that it is merely one of the mystery religions of the Fertile Crescent?

What about Holy Communion? Is that unique to Christianity? Why, the priests of Mithraism slit the throat of the bull and drank the blood. What about a risen Savior? All the mystery religions had a dead-god theme. It was man's way of explaining the seasonal changes of the earth, death in the winter and resurrection in the spring.

Doubt crept into my soul. Was the life and death and resurrection of Jesus just another fable similar to that of Persephone, abducted into the underworld but allowed to return for eight months to renew the earth? How You must grieve to observe young minds being seduced by the siren song of doubt and to see them crashing on the rocks of unbelief.

In psychology class, the siren song grew louder. Discussing the instability of puberty, professors quoted statistics on the ecstatic religious experiences of youth from the ages of twelve through eighteen. I had had one of those ecstatic religious experiences, but in college I lost that certainty of knowing Your voice and Your presence. Was that experience real or not? Perhaps it was a psychological phenomenon. Maybe it was merely excess hormones bumping into loose nerve endings, and I shorted out.

I thought I knew Your voice, but those college voices swirled in my head.

"Life is pain. Nirvana is the cessation of pain, as a burning candle snuffed out."

"God is everything. He is the tree, the flower, the cow. The goal of life is to be freed from your individuality by being absorbed into the All."

"God is dead. There is no meaning in life except what a person forges for himself."

My childhood faith protested, "The Bible reveals a loving God who walked and talked with people."

More liberated and enlightened students tried to set me straight: "You naïve, fundamentalist Christians. You sing your saccharin songs depicting a god walking and talking with you in the garden and chucking you under the chin. How can you believe in a personal god who involves himself in the mundane affairs of human beings? There may be some supreme intelligence, but don't expect that superior mind to care about your hangnail. You surely don't believe in a literal interpretation of the Bible, do you? It is merely an allegory to try to explain life as viewed by an ancient culture. Don't be taken in by talk of heaven and hell, either. There is no after-life."

I wrestled with the denial of eternal life. Although as a child my own life seemed to stretch far into the distance, I knew the reality of death. When she was only seven, my mother had lost her mother to pneumonia. In my little country church, I had attended numerous funerals, where we had sung of life on the other side. Living on a farm, I saw life and death up close with the birth of farm animals and pets and then the abrupt death at butchering time and as the result of accidents related to heavy farm equipment.

Death was a cruel finality. Perhaps the songs of heaven were only soothing medication poured into the wounds of grief without any basis in reality. After all, I never had had any proof of life beyond the grave. Of course, the Bible was full of assurances, but if it were only an allegory, then could I really base my hopes on these assurances?

Near the end of my college years, my hope was fading. I mentally joined the ranks of unbelievers. I concluded that the only immortality possible was a material recycling. If one were lucky enough to decompose under a tree, then he or she could make good compost, causing the tree to thrive until it also died and decayed, fertilizing another plant. But, on the other hand, what if the spiritual part of human beings does continue to exist?

Lord, I was so confused. The battle between my mind and my spirit raged on. Eventually my mind surrendered to the lies of man, but my spirit clung to Your truth. Deep inside, Your message lay dormant until the crises of life forced open the grave maintained by "vain imaginations."

In the summer before my senior year, terminal cancer stalked our home. At the age of forty-eight my father lay in a coma in the hospital. Kneeling in the chapel, I begged You to spare his life. But my mind taunted me: "God's not listening. He's not even there. Why pick up the phone to place a call if no one is on the other end to answer you?"

My spirit struggled to rise above the suffocating doubts to recapture my childhood trust in You. I read the Scriptures. I said the healing prayers. To my great sorrow, my father died, but his death opened the gates of heaven for me.

On the morning that Daddy died, he rallied from a two-week coma, leaned forward, and began to sing. Although Mother could not make out the words, she knew it was a hymn. She shared with my sister and me that he seemed to glow with a radiant light and looked beyond her into a world she could not see. I remember thinking, *There is life after death. There is a God in heaven. And I had better get my hand in His before the next crisis hits.*

O, Lord, You are so patient. You rekindled the embers of my dying faith, but I failed to tend the fire. The embers grew cold. I didn't intend to ignore Your gift, and I grieve that I disappointed You. Although You extended Your hand to me, I was reluctant to entrust myself fully to You yet. I had an agenda of my own—a thesis to write, a wedding to plan, then graduate school, and teaching. But You knew that life would bring struggles that would propel me right into Your arms...and You waited.

# CHAPTER 2

# Darkness and Depression

The "next crisis" hit and hit hard. I hesitate to go back there. Please hold my hand, Lord, as I revisit that year of depression. It is so dark here. Thick blackness lurks in my peripheral vision every time I awaken. I can almost touch it. My head is heavy and I dread to lift it from the pillow. The air is heavy also, making breathing difficult. Everything is difficult. Energy has drained from my body. I no longer trip down the stairs to start a new day. I drag my body from the bed and shuffle through my chores.

Chores. Life is a chore. I even have to will my hand to hold a teacup and force my other hand to wash it. I am so slow. Yes, a woman's work is never done, but mine has become a mountain that towers over me, defying me to conquer it. Maybe I never will. Maybe I will always be a failure. Clutter piles up around me. My unkempt house has become a reflection of my cluttered mind. Thoughts race through my head, zigzagging back and forth, chasing each other in tangled circles.

*How did I get here? How do I get out?* I must have entered one of those crazy houses at the carnival, full of mazes, dead-ends, and no exits. Accusing voices taunt me:

*So this is where the valedictorian of the class ended up. So much for your education. You can't even balance the checkbook.*

*What if the people in your husband's church would drop in for an unexpected visit? How could you make all of the unfolded laundry disappear? What if they would hear you screaming at the kids? You're such a saint on Sunday but a witch on Monday.*

*You're in a crazy house with no exit. Maybe there is one exit, a final exit. Maybe the children and David would be better off without you. He could find an efficient housekeeper and a calm, capable mother.*

*If you don't get it together, your children are going to be warped for life.*

God, where are you? Make these voices stop. I've tried to get help. I told my family doctor that I needed something for my nerves. His advice was to stop bottling up my frustrations and let them have expression. What a mistake. It was like shaking up a seltzer water, uncorking it, and spraying all of its contents on the whole family. I even threw a cup against the wall in an attempt to release some pressure. That surely was a help. Just another mess to clean up.

I can never forget the bewildered, frightened look in the children's eyes. As hard as I try, I cannot get the cork back in the bottle. I have released an angry genie. I am screaming at the children and constantly complaining to my poor husband. Where do I go from here, God? Are You up there? Do You hear me? Do You care? Do You have a plan?

My husband has a plan. He's taking me to counseling. I lost it this morning. He came down the stairs to see his out-of-control wife standing in the middle of the kitchen, holding her head, and screaming at the top of her lungs. All of this in front of two wide-eyed, beautiful children sitting in their high-chairs. I know I need help and I am ready. Yes, I will go with David to see our pastoral counselor. I have to.

One visit to Dr. Williams has left me swimming in a sea of questions and scary emotions. Why don't I want to face them? All of his probing questions have pried the lid off my carefully locked box of insecurity and resentments. I don't want to look at them.

Often awakened as a child by my mother's sweet song, "Good morning, merry sunshine," I took on a cheery persona. I lived to make others happy, to bring sunshine into their lives. I didn't throw tantrums. I was a good little girl, and that brought me much affirmation. I didn't let myself get angry. That would have ruined my own image of who I was and threatened my reputation as the sweet little sunshine girl.

But now the storms of life are threatening to blow away that sunshine façade. I can still keep the mask on during Sunday services and in front of my in-laws and acquaintances, but the front is beginning to crack. I've tried to tell my mother some of my turmoil, but she can't believe what she is hearing from her "positive, got-it-together daughter." She can't fathom the fact that I'm struggling with so much anger and confusion.

Oh, God, help me. I try to hide from the storm. I want to escape the pressure, but nothing helps. I can't go enough places, read enough novels, take enough naps. The fact is, I can't escape because I cannot escape myself. I can't take this torment, and I can't let my family suffer because of my confusion.

Dr. Williams is right. The anger that I let out of that uncorked bottle is aimed at the wrong people. I don't have the courage to confront other people who wound me, and I let the bottled-up frustration come out at home. It's time to be open and honest and face my fears, mostly my anger.

So at whom am I angry? Might as well start at the top. I'm angry at You, God. I don't like the way you made me. I don't like my body. Why couldn't You have given me a beautiful body instead of this scrawny, skinny frame? Growing up, some kids called me "Skeleton!" "Toothpick!" "The running gears of a katydid!" All of these darts pierced my heart and left deep wounds, but I never let the pain show. Trying to deflect the embarrassment and tears inside, I joined the game, laughing and calling myself names.

But home alone, I cried. How I envied girls with shapely legs. I have bird-legs, and worse yet, they are bowed. I rarely wear shorts and am always glad when the hemlines are long. You could have saved me a great deal of pain by giving me a different body. Then maybe I wouldn't have been so vulnerable to other people's opinions and become such an expert people-pleaser.

Pleasing people is a dangerous trap. It robs me of my self-respect and self expression. I can't be myself. I dare not tell people what I really think. I must keep my anger to myself for fear that they might not like me. And being liked is vital to survival. I can't live with disapproval.

That's why I can't have an open, honest relationship with my mother- and father-in-law. I want them to like me and think of me as a good wife and mother. I always comply with their wishes, even when I don't want to and don't agree with their opinions—especially in regard to rearing our children. And that's becoming more of a problem.

I want to shout loudly and clearly that they are not the parents, but I'm afraid of hurting their feelings.

They are wonderful, giving people. I'm sure they don't realize that they are infringing on my role and authority. Besides, when I once tried to discuss my differences with them, they were both hurt. I can't risk a disruption with them. I need their affirmation.

At least I've admitted my anger to myself, to my husband, and to the counselor. That's given me a valve to release some steam from my internal pressure cooker. What a relief to know that I'm not about to blow the lid completely off. That would be messy!

Facing and admitting my anger is bringing me freedom. Denying and burying it caused me mental and emotional pain. I need to be honest and transparent. First John 1:9 makes that very clear: "If we claim to be without sin, we deceive ourselves and the truth is not in us. If we confess our sins, he is faithful and just and will forgive us our sins and purify us from all unrighteousness" (NIV). Lord, you can't forgive and free me if I refuse to face and confess my faults.

I might as well be honest about my frustrations of being a pastor's wife. Living up to the congregation's expectations is stressful. It really is like living in a fishbowl. I know how the people in my church at home talked about the pastor and his family. Perhaps because they paid the pastor's salary, they thought they had the right to pass judgment on everything from the behavior of their children to the way they spent their money. It seemed to me as if they thought they owned them.

I got a taste of being owned during my husband's summer pastorate in seminary days. The church generously offered to furnish the empty parsonage with some of their extra things. One lady brought me some paper draperies, relics of the 1950s, I imagine. She also brought her pair of pinking shears because she knew I would want to give them a finishing touch of pinked edges.

Well, I didn't want pinked edges and politely declined her offer to do it for me. I thought I had made it clear that I preferred the drapes just as they were, but as she left, she mentioned that she was leaving the shears because she knew I would change my mind and didn't want me to have to drive to her house to get them. At the end of the summer, the drapes remained untouched, just as I wanted them. I hope I returned the shears. I know I felt a surge of pride in my resolve. I had stood my ground.

Now I can't say no to anyone in the church. I don't have any backbone enabling me to take a stand. I bake cookies and pies when I don't have time and I give devotional lessons when I don't want to. I go to church when I don't want to. And resentment begins to grow. Sometimes I don't like the person I am becoming.

# CHAPTER 3

# Identity Crisis

During every counseling session, Dr. Williams presses me further to peel back the layers camouflaging my anger, fostering a growing depression. He is forcing me to be brutally honest. Yes, there is suppressed anger in my life. Yes, there is frustration. Yes, there is confusion. I don't know who I am anymore. I used to be Mrs. Schramm—respected and confident English teacher—but that identity is gone.

Who am I now? Pastor's wife, mother of two children seventeen months apart, and an amorphous blob trying to cope with dirty dishes, mounds of laundry, clutter, and runny noses—not to mention all of those rank dirty diapers simmering in the pail. What was it Dr. Minar said when I showed him my engagement ring at the beginning of my senior year in college? "Another scholar down the drain." Right. The truth of that statement never rings truer than when I am flushing feces from dirty diapers.

What happened to my dream of becoming a professor of English literature? Yes, I know. I chose to get married. I chose to decline my acceptance into the doctoral program at Northwestern University to follow David to Harvard. I chose to have children. I love my children. They're wonderful, beautiful, and bright. I chose to be a homemaker. I should be a good one. I had six years of home economics and eight years of 4-H. I just didn't know that juggling everything would be so hard. I chose all of these roles, but I did not choose to become a pastor's wife.

Pastor's wife. Ah, there's the rub. My marvelously intelligent husband pulled a bait-and-switch trick on me. When we were engaged, he was going to become a professor of psychology. Months before we were married, he decided to follow an inner nudge to go to seminary. Following seminary, he chose to go to Harvard for a doctorate in Old Testament Studies and Biblical Languages. After one year of the doctoral program and the birth of our first child, he left Harvard to answer a call to pastoral ministry.

Pastoral ministry? I didn't sign up to be a pastor's wife. I still have issues with the church. I had always gone to church, even during my years of spiritual confusion in college, but it had become just a habit. I couldn't get answers for my agonizing questions of why good people have to suffer and why I couldn't connect with the God that I had given my life to as a young girl.

Yes, You are right, Lord. After I had a glimpse of You and Your promise of eternal life at the time of my father's death, I actually buried all of my questions and put my search for You on hold. I had intended to get my hand in Yours before the next crisis hit, but I didn't. Now the crisis is here. I am a seething cauldron of anger. I am angry with you, God. I am angry with the church. I am angry with my husband for entering the pastoral ministry. I am angry with everyone I feel obligated to please. I am angry with myself for getting into such a mess.

Not only am I angry, God; I am afraid. Depression has brought darkness, and in that darkness I feel lost. I don't know where I am going. Where is the light? If only I could be free of this stifling, heavy cloud. Staggering in confusion without direction, I stumble through the day. I used to be able to organize my thoughts. Now I can't control the dizzying anxieties that surge through my mind.

Numbly I force myself to outline my routine for the day, but interruptions send everything spiraling out of control. Phone calls, unexpected visits, and whimpering children demanding to have their needs met pull me into the vortex of a swirling whirlpool. When can I break free and drift into a quiet eddy for renewal?

All day long I give pieces of myself away. Then I can't pull myself together, not correctly anyway. I feel like "Mrs. Potato Head" assembled by a two-year old with my feet in my mouth, my lips on my ears, and my nose on top of my head. There I go, slipping into self pity; that's another pit. "Pit," "swamp," "quagmire," and "whirlpool" all express my sense of entrapment. When will I break free? Oh, God, do You hear me? When will You help me find the key to my freedom?

Here it is 3:00 a.m., and I am in the living room huddled beside the radio with a flashlight and map, tracking the path of a tornado sighted somewhere southwest of us. The lights are still out. I don't want my husband to know I'm stressing over this. He went to bed, trusting You, God. I wish I could be more trusting, but I keep remembering the tornado that ripped through our community in my childhood, killing one of my schoolmates.

But what would I do if I heard the train-roar of an approaching twister? I surely wouldn't go to that damp, creepy cellar. I saw a dead rat the only time I ventured down there. Some people suggest a ditch as a safe place, but I'd be afraid of snakes or scary night creatures.

Why do bad storms have to come in the night? That makes them twice as scary. Whew! The funnel cloud must have lifted. The warning has been cancelled. Now I am limp and emotionally spent. Sleep-deprived again,

I will have to stumble through the day, trying to meet the needs of my rested, energetic children.

Fear is a hard-taskmaster. Not only is fear a tyrant; it is also pervasive, with tentacles reaching into many areas of my life. Nightmares of losing our children through all sorts of horrible diseases and accidents crush me in the night. In turn, I smother those fear-free little chicks under my hovering wings. Then I dread the thought that I may be infusing their psyches with fear, crippling them for life.

And what if I should die prematurely, would David find a mate to love them as her own? Or if David should die, how would I support the family? I certainly wouldn't want to work outside the home, leaving my impressionable little ones with a sitter. As one young mother said to me, "I didn't have children to see them grow up like their babysitter. I want to leave my imprint on their lives."

But what kind of imprint am I making? I certainly don't want them to become carbon copies of this confused creature. Right now I don't like myself. I'm actually afraid of myself. How bizarre! I'm afraid of myself! I fear the volatile emotions that erupt unexpectedly. How long will I be able to hold my anger and exasperations in check? Will the day come when I lose control and attack my own offspring? Never in my wildest dreams could I conceive of abusing a small child.

Now I understand. Just the other day I found myself pummeling a pillow substitute. I am a ticking time bomb, a live grenade, about to explode. There is no quiet place to deprogram this lethal device. Voices inside and out drive me crazy. My head nearly bursts with tormenting accusations and self condemnation, and the children babble all the time.

Will there ever come a time when every thought that enters their minds ceases to shoot out of their mouths? Nonstop verbiage. Nonstop demands. There's always that last request that sets me off and I scream: "What? What do you want now?" Worse than the constant demands are the squabbles. Do I have to be a referee, too? No doubt any mother of more than one child should be issued a striped shirt and a whistle.

Confused within, I carry my confusion wherever I go—even to church. On the surface I portray the sweet little pastor's wife pitching in to help wherever I can, but inwardly I am frustrated. I want more. I long for answers for my search for victorious Christian living. There has to be more than I am experiencing.

I am desperate to know if Christianity actually works in the trenches of everyday life; therefore, in Sunday School classes I ask questions that are perhaps too personal. "Does your faith make a difference in the way you do your job? Does it make you a better employee? How does it affect the way you interact with your associates? How does it affect your family life?"

Not only do I badger the teacher with questions; I also am guilty of harassing the pastor. I'm sure he doesn't need the stress of a struggling, probing wife. Yet he listens patiently while I pour out my disappointment with the church.

What makes the church different from the many service clubs? They offer the same fellowship and interdependence, and they even reach out to those in need. They have a chaplain who leads in prayer and in devotions. I don't see much difference. Kiwanis, Rotary, Presbyterian, United Methodist—it's a toss-up.

No wonder people say that they don't need church. To me the church seems impotent. If anyone has a major problem, the church has to refer them to a professional outside the church. Where is the power of the early church that turned the world upside down? I just want to know if there is a place on this planet where the dynamic accounts of changed lives in the New Testament are being re-enacted today? Is Christianity still vitally alive anywhere?

Yes, yes. A resounding yes! Christianity does change lives, even today. I may not see it in a dramatic way in my small world, but I have just read an exciting account of the power of Christianity in the lives of desperate men. Thank you, God, for answering my desperate cry for meaning and for validating Christianity for me through Ernest Gordon's exciting book, *Through the Valley of the Quai.*

I have just read vivid accounts of men reduced to the level of animals fighting for survival, stealing from and betraying each other during their internment in the Japanese death camps. But the loving sacrifices of a few Christians restored their God-given dignity, and secret prayer and Bible study gave them strength to love and befriend their tormentors, defeating the evil that had been destroying them.

Thank You, God. There is hope for me. Christianity is real. Jesus is alive and active on this planet. Now I just have to get my hand in His. My step is lighter now. I really do have hope. I am beginning to anticipate something good about to happen.

Another exciting book! "There is no frigate like a book to take us lands away...."[1] Whatever the destination was for Emily Dickinson, the destination for me is miles away from darkness and hopelessness—a way out of the crazy carnival house of confusing mazes and warped mirrors.

Teen Challenge Ministry is coming to our little town and has sent advanced copies of David Wilkerson's *The Cross and the Switchblade.* Here is an account of a man in our time walking and talking with You, Lord. I mean actually talking—a two-way conversation. He's getting feedback. He's getting answers. He's seeing results in the radically changed lives of gang members in New York City.

At first I asked myself, "Who does he think he is anyway? He sends up a request, and bam, the answer comes on a silver platter. He asks for direct signs to help him make a decision, and he gets them. He prays for $500 to keep his ministry afloat for one more week, and checks arrive in the mail to cover the exact amount." (I'm jealous!)

I want that kind of relationship with You, God. I want that kind of interaction. I want to walk and talk with You in the cool of the day just as Adam and Eve did. Now that I know that that level of communication is still possible, I'm going to find it. I am going to escape this confusion.

Thank You, God, for *The Cross and the Switchblade*'s taking me a few steps out of the darkness toward the light. Now, You are asking me to take a few more steps. It's only a short distance to the altar of my husband's little country church, but it seems like a mile. He's been challenged by David Wilkerson's ministry to call people to active faith. He's asking anyone who wants to make a first-time commitment or a recommitment to Christ to step forward.

He doesn't know that he is talking to his own wife. The congregation doesn't know he's talking to the pastor's wife, either. What will they think? Well, it doesn't matter what they think. It matters what You think.

Because the children weren't well, I didn't go to the Teen Challenge meetings and make a public recommitment. But You've been drawing me to Yourself during these ensuing weeks. You've been orchestrating events. I know You have. Those two enlightening books didn't fall into my hands by chance. I can feel my heart pounding inside my chest. I have to answer Your call. I have to step out.

What a relief that the congregation didn't judge me harshly—in fact, they welcomed my confession of my drifting away from You and my longing to reconnect. Perhaps David was a little surprised, but he's getting used to my surprises. Now I don't feel like a hypocrite. I've taken off the mask of religiosity and I'm becoming more transparent. I don't have to be perfect. I am forgiven. I am free.

I'm still struggling with some issues in the church. I still have questions, but the big question has been answered. I know that You, God, are not an impersonal being untouched by human suffering. You are not the eternal watchmaker, winding up the earth and flinging it into space to function on its own. You are a loving creator who wants to interact with Your creation.

Yes, Lord, I know that You want to interact with me. You love me! And that makes all the difference. I have a new identity. I am chosen. I am worthy. I have a purpose. Lord, I accept the challenge to love You with all of my heart and to love my neighbor as myself. I also accept being a pastor's wife.

# CHAPTER 4

# A New Challenge

Lord, I've accepted the challenge of being a pastor's wife, but I'm not sure I am up to the challenge of another pregnancy so soon. This can't be happening to me! Three babies in three years! How can I manage? I'm just beginning to cope better with the two that I have. Our youngest has recently turned one. We're all sleeping again, and I am beginning to feel like a normal human being instead of the zombie that shuffled through this house. Lord, I love children, but this is just not good timing!

Maysel's visit wasn't good timing, either. I had just lost my breakfast, a very intriguing spectacle for the children, and they didn't miss one frame of the action as they reran the film for my friend from the church. They eagerly announced, "This is what Mommy does." Then they both sprang into action.

Fanning themselves, they rushed to the back door to get fresh air. This obviously wasn't a satisfactory solution since they clapped one hand over their mouths, rushed to grab a bowl from the shelf, and began dramatically heaving. Turning to me, Maysel said knowingly, "Oh, really?" The secret is out: an early release by our two young actors.

I wish I could act as if nothing is bothering me. I haven't come to terms with another pregnancy yet, and now I have to deal with other people's opinions and inane comments. "Don't you two know what causes this condition?" "You must be very fertile." Even men in the church feel free to harass David, as they make jokes about his virility.

I don't know why a pregnancy becomes everyone else's business. All too soon people will begin patting my belly and commenting on my size. "What? You're only six months along? Why, you look as if you could deliver any day." Then they will start asking that most annoying question: "Are you still here? I thought you'd have gone to the hospital long before this." Lord, I need some peace.

Thank You, Lord, for the interpersonal sharing group for pastoral couples led by our counselor. Even if we have to drive an hour for the sessions, it is worth it. I've found a safe place to vent and reflect. The months are passing quickly, and true to form, I'm getting larger and larger. Some women can carry their babies discreetly, but I seem to shove them right out front for all to see and even bump into.

I'm thankful to have supportive friends who allow me to weep and blurt out my frustration. I get so angry when even waitresses look accusingly at my bulging belly and then at my toddlers and say, "Are these all yours?" People act as if our children are taking up their space or breathing their air. I remember the descendant of Aldous Huxley admonishing us as upcoming college graduates not to have children but to buy a television instead. Overpopulation. And we're guilty.

Thank, You, Lord, for absolution and affirmation from a dear Lutheran pastor. He loves our children and demonstrates that with abandon. Our Jeannie greets him at the door with, "Good afternoon, Pastor Keifer. How you do day?"

Captivated by her, he sits right down on the floor and engages in animated conversation with her. He quickly dismisses the comments of implied crimes against the planet and society by saying, "Your children are bright and adorable. Our society needs the kind of citizens your home will produce."

Now I can pat my belly and say, "Welcome soon, little one. You are a gift to this world and to me." Psalm 127:3-4 (NIV) says it best: "Sons [and daughters] are a heritage from the Lord, children a reward from him.... Blessed is the man whose quiver is full of them."

Thank You for being my shield and my friend and for giving me solace. A few short months ago, I was filled with frustration, anxiety, and a little dread. Now I am filled with peace, hope, and even anticipation. Well, to be honest, I'm not looking forward to labor. I'm ready to welcome a new baby, but I'm so tired. Running after two creative toddlers, rather, "lumbering" after two toddlers, has left me drained of energy.

When I told the doctor of my misgivings, he assured me that he would be with me all the way and would be sure to make me comfortable. He plans to give me a spinal block, making even the final stages of labor pain free. That's a relief.

Just two weeks to go, and I think I'm ready. Baby clothes washed. Check. Bassinet ready. Check. Changing table equipped with supplies. Check. Diaper service ordered. Check. Pain-free labor and delivery arranged. Check. Okay, Mama's here to help with the children while David is at youth camp for a week, and I'm feeling more relaxed. When Daddy gets home from camp, Little One, we are set to go.

Oh, no, Lord, not yet. It's 1:30 in the morning and I'm suddenly awake. My water cannot be breaking now. David is still three hours away at the church campground. Who will stay with the children? Who will take me to the hospital? I've counted on David being with me as he was with my other two deliveries. I remember how calm he's always been, even quietly graphing the frequency and intensity of my contractions. I need him now. I want him now!

Well, he is not here and I will have to depend on prayer. Jesus, help me to trust in You and not panic. I'll call the campground soon. Mama can stay with the children. I have friends who can drive me to the hospital. I hate to go too soon, but my nurse friend, Janet, may be right. I'm carrying this baby very low, and, being a third delivery, the labor may be quick.

Yep, I'm definitely losing amniotic fluid, and I'm becoming uncomfortable. Time to awaken Mama and think of my options for assistance. Must leave a message for David. The camp director won't appreciate a phone call at this hour, but this is the camp emergency number and this is sort of an emergency.

Thank, You, Lord. All is going smoothly. My friend Janet has come to stay with the children, and Gertrude is taking both Mama and me to the hospital. I've called the hospital, and they're going to alert the doctor. Hopefully David will make it on time.

Lord, this is definitely not what I had expected. Because of so many women in labor today, I have been stuck in this "overflow" room filled with hospital supplies. Not the most desirable room, but at least there is a bed, and I am being prepped. Hospital policy forbids anyone but the husband in the labor room. Rats! Can't have Mama with me. I hope David makes it soon.

Things are progressing much faster than I had anticipated. Where is David? Let's see. I called the camp director at 3:00 a.m. It takes approximately three hours. Oh, my, it's 8:00 a.m. What could have happened? He's overdue.

Well, I'm certainly not overdue. I'm early and thrusting toward delivery time. How could labor have intensified so fast? These contractions are something else. Where is my doctor? I haven't even seen him yet. "With me all the way." Right. "Enough meds to keep me comfortable." Right.

The nurse hasn't even stuck her head in the door since she prepped me. I am completely alone. Oh, God, I'm scared. I need somebody. I wish I had practiced the Lamaze method, but I didn't plan to have to use it. These contractions are getting more intense. I know I'm not breathing right—in fact, I think I'm working against the process. I am so tense. I feel my body recoiling from the pain. I think I'm hyperventilating. I can't breathe. I feel light-headed. Very little time between contractions. What if I pass out?

Lord, help! Jesus, is that You? Yes, oh, yes. What a clear, comforting voice is resonating within me: "Let Me take you through this." Yes, Lord, yes. I will. Halleluiah! I am not alone! You are here. You heard me.

You saw me. You care. You are talking to me. You really are talking to me. Awesome! You want to be my coach. Thank You. Thank You. Thank You. Now I am relaxing. I am breathing more smoothly. I can feel the rhythm. I can do this thing with Your help. We are a good team.

Thank, You, Lord, for repeating Your instructions every time I've started to tense up and gotten out of rhythm. You really are a good coach. It's marvelous to think that the creator of the universe is supervising my labor. Amazing. Lord, I will never forget this day. I will never forget Your words to me. I will never again doubt that You are the God who interacts with His people.

I wonder how much time has passed? The clock says 8:30 a.m. I forgot all about my call button. And it's time. I think I'm ready to push more than just the call button. I hope the nurse comes fast. No nurse. Just an aide. I told her I needed the nurse because I'm ready to deliver.

Message from the nurse: "Can't be, honey. Your labor has stopped." Oh, no, it hasn't. Jesus, please bring me some help. Here she is. "Let's take a look. Oh, no— there's the head! Quick! Check on a delivery room while I call the doctor. I told him to enjoy a leisurely breakfast because nothing was happening. Hang in there, Honey! Don't push!"

Thank You for keeping me calm in this whirlwind of activity, Jesus. No chance for much instruction. Eased onto a gurney and rushed to a delivery room by a frantic nurse and her aide, I'm grateful that I could remember the pattern of shallow breathing to stall the actual birthing.

Now I've been passed off to a frazzled delivery room nurse, who is scurrying about collecting necessary supplies in anticipation of the doctor's arrival. "Hold steady on that delivery table, Sweetheart. Don't move about. I haven't secured everything yet. And if the doctor delays much longer and you can't hold back, let me know and I'll be there with you. I've called for an intern."

Well, the intern came, the doctor came, and the baby came. After all of that frantic flurry, I can relax. My beautiful baby girl is in my arms, and my husband is finally at my side. Deep inside there is a new peace. Almighty God, you have visited me. The pain and confusion were worth having the opportunity to hear Your voice and sense Your presence. I know that You are the God who comes.

Thank you, God, for coming. I am humbled and in awe that You entered into my world of pain and panic and brought peace. How can it be that in the midst of major world problems that You could be aware of me? You really are all-knowing. You really do love every particle of Your creation. Your vastness overwhelms me. Please help me hang onto the Truth that I have encountered. I know You are faithful.

There is one question though. Did You set me up to have to depend on You? Why did the camp director wait to deliver my message to David until breakfast, when he knew I was going to the hospital in the early hours of the morning? Why did I go into labor on one of the busiest days in the birthing unit? Why did the nurse think that my labor had stopped? Who wrote that on my chart?

I may never have those answers, but I do know that You saw me and loved me and chose to intervene in my life. Thank You. Thank You.

# CHAPTER 5

# Desperate for a Consistent Walk

Here I am again, God, desperate for Your help. Months have passed, and I have lost that place of intimacy with You. I didn't intend to let that happen. I promised to spend time in prayer and Bible study, but I have failed. Right now I'm just trying to survive amidst the constant demands.

I'm too rushed in the mornings to give You more than a salute as I begin the battle of the day, and I'm so tired at night that I mumble a brief prayer and am usually asleep before David finishes the Bible reading. At least I have to stay awake when it's my turn to read, but I'm sure I don't absorb much.

I am so sorry. I am just like the Israelites, wandering away from You, falling into a pit, crying out, experiencing Your rescue, only to wander away again. I was like that as a little girl, praying desperately for Your protection during a storm in the night and promising never again to disobey You or my parents. Then when the sun came up in the morning, I lacked the strength to keep those promises.

As a young person at a camp or conference, I would go up the mountain, encounter Your presence, and return home glowing. Then after two weeks when the glow would go, I would be back in the valley of doubts and indifference. Why can't I be faithful?

"If we are faithless, he will remain faithful, for he cannot disown himself" (2 Timothy 2:13, NIV). Thank You, Lord. That verse gives me hope that You will never give up on me. You still keep sending encouragement. Maybe someday I will become like David Wilkerson in *The Cross and the Switchblade*, always walking with You, becoming strong and bold and even helping others.

I often wondered where his strength came from. He kept talking about the Holy Spirit. As United Methodists, we talk about the Holy Spirit in the liturgy, and we read the account in Acts of His coming on the day of Pentecost. But we never talk much of interacting with Him on a daily basis.

I guess I don't understand the Holy Spirit. Another thing I don't understand is the account of a life-altering experience of one of the drug addicts in The Cross and the Switchblade. I remember reading that Maria, who had met Jesus, also met the Holy Spirit. Then one day, she called David Wilkerson to exclaim that "it" had happened. Rivers of living water were flowing out of her. What in the world did that mean?

Jesus, You have all the answers, and You send the right messenger at the right time. One of David's high school classmates came to visit and hand-delivered the answer to my recent questions in John Sherrill's *They Speak With Other Tongues.* She had worked with the Teen Challenge Ministry in Pennsylvania and was excited to share her discoveries. What a perfect follow-up to our own encounter with Teen Challenge through *The Cross and the Switchblade.* I was hungry and gobbled up every morsel that she offered.

There were a few things that I couldn't quite stomach though—namely her "Hallelujahs" and "Praise the Lords." Every time she uttered them, I felt myself stiffen and draw back. Although the language was unfamiliar, the message was just what I was seeking, and I could not wait to devour the truth in this new book as soon as our heaven-sent visitor was on her way. Jesus, Your timing is perfect.

Eureka! I've found it. I've found it! The missing element in my Christian walk: the Holy Spirit! David Wilkerson spoke as if everyone knows the Holy Spirit as a person. I don't. Now John Sherrill has introduced Him to me.

That's not quite correct. I've been given a thorough resume, but I have yet to encounter Him. Thanks to Sherrill's thorough investigation of the Holy Spirit's role in Scripture and throughout history, I am not dreading that encounter—in fact, I can't wait! Now I just have to find a group of Christians to help facilitate that encounter.

It's a good thing another spiritual event is coming soon. I'm barely hanging onto the cliff of the last mountaintop experience. Truthfully, I fell off weeks ago, and I'm slogging through the mire of the mundane. Caring for three babies within three years can take the shine off the best saint's halo. The problem with motherhood is that it is so daily! Sort of like that game of Aggravation: every time I think I'm about to reach a goal, I'm sent back to start all over again.

Thank You, Lord, that I can laugh, or I would be in an asylum by now. Just the other day I saw all of my clean, folded laundry rolling on the floor wrapped around two hysterical toddlers. Later another batch of laundry paraded past on our eldest who had layered herself in every clean little dress she could pull over her head. What a sight she was, with her arms sticking straight out like broomsticks from an overstuffed scarecrow. I don't know how she did it.

She is a very skillful, creative little girl. Not seeing anything to sweep with her new little broom and dustpan, she emptied the entire contents of a potato flakes box on the floor. Voila! A mess to clean up! That was easier for Mommy than the shortening scooped into my pots and pans and diligently stirred by my little chef and her brother. I was just in time to rescue a dozen eggs from the same culinary artist.

Jeannie loves sensory experiences with food—especially chocolate. While diapering her brother in a nearby room, I became concerned about the quiet in the kitchen and asked, "Jeannie, what are you doing?"

"Pouring," answered a little voice.

"Pouring what?"

"Nummy," came the reply. Finishing the diaper as quickly as possible, I rushed into the kitchen to find her slurping chocolate syrup from a puddle on the chair. What a sight: chocolate dripping from a cute goatee on her chin onto her pink fuzzy jammies and pooling onto the floor. What could I do except take a picture?

Humor saved us both the other day when she concocted another horrific mess. This time it was in her bed during a supposed nap. Peeking through the crack of a nearly closed door, I was astounded to see Jeannie sifting through a huge pile of potting soil, vermiculite, decapitated flowers, and the shredded contents of an entire box of tissues, all of which she had purloined from the dresser adjacent to her bed.

After gaining my composure, I asked, "What shall we do with Jeannie?" Her response completely disarmed me.

"Well, we could spank her, or we could love her. If we spank her, she will cry; so I guess we'll just have to love her." And we did. A sudden flashback of my childhood bewilderment when my attempts to be creatively helpful were rewarded with spankings spared her the same fate. How could I have helped my mother darn my new red socks if I hadn't cut the toes off first? Like mother, like daughter.

But there are days when there is no humor in squabbling siblings, dirty dishes, and dirty diapers from three children. Our three-year-old will no longer sit on the potty chair. After all, brother and sister are getting regular attention during diaper changes. Why should she miss out? My resolve to be a patient parent is weakening. I am so tired. My thinking is fuzzy and I sense the fog of confusion creeping back into my life.

God, You've got to help me. I can't make it on my own. I lack the inner strength. I need You. I need Your presence within me, beside me, all around me. I have to have the infilling of the Holy Spirit that David Wilkerson talked about. I want to be like Maria in *The Cross and the Switchblade*, rescued from her old lifestyle and empowered to live a changed life. I fool myself thinking I am so holy, but I am no better than girls like Maria. I've never taken drugs. I've never robbed or stabbed anyone, but I have the same capacity for evil within me. Yes, that's true. I have to admit it.

The problem is *self*. I try to portray the image of a selfless wife and mother devoted to sacrificing for husband and children, but the bottom line is self survival, comfort, and pleasure. I still want what I want and when I want it. I want sleep. I want rest. I want peace and quiet in the house. When I don't get that, I become frustrated and irritable. I quickly deny the anger, but it doesn't go away. Instead it festers inside, erupting at the next provocation.

Just the other day, I was too rough in my intervention between Jeannie and Mark. She persisted in trying to make him do what she wanted even after several warnings. Annoyed by the bickering, I angrily pulled her away, causing her to lose her balance and fall. What if she had struck her temple on the play table? Guilt and remorse plagued me.

I still have the capacity for great evil. I thought I had changed. I am afraid of myself again. I felt relief that I didn't have to be a hypocrite any longer, but how can I confess scenes like this to the congregation? That's my problem with the church. We deny our depravity and thus fail to experience restoration.

All the way to church, our children squabble, and I scream at them. Then we pull into the church parking lot and put on our smiling masks, greeting other plastic smiles, hiding who knows what. Oh, Lord, help us to be real. Help us to deal with our depravity. Placed in another environment, such as gang-infested slums, we could become the very people we judge so harshly with our scorn.

# CHAPTER 6

# A Vision and a Promise

Lord, help me to be honest about my spiritual state with the pastors and their wives when we meet together to prepare ourselves for the community-wide evangelistic crusade with Ford Philpot. He wants to deal with sin in the church before he confronts sin in the community.

Well, there surely is sin in my heart. I resent this whole affair. For a month my husband has been in Saturday training sessions with the advance team of the Philpot ministry. Saturday morning is my one time of relief, because that is the only day David is not rushing off to minister or administrate. Sometimes I feel as if the ministry is his mistress taking him away from me. Now I have had to deal with a second ministry mistress. I'm jealous and I'm witchy. Can't bring myself to spell that with a "b." Still in pretense mode.

The time has come to confront pretense and hypocrisy. I'm sitting here with the community pastors and spouses, being asked to deal with barriers to God's visitation, either personal or denominational. We've been asked to voice our failings in prayer.

I've listened to confessions of prayerlessness, etc., and now I hear myself blurting out, "I'm angry at this whole project because it has taken my husband away from me when I need him desperately on Saturday mornings. Ministry robs parsonage families of time and normalcy. As a pastor's wife, I have to confess jealousy of the church.

And another thing: I have to confess frustration at my own inability to successfully live the Christian life. I need help. I'm tired of being a yo-yo Christian, always up and down, never making permanent progress. I get right with God, walk a few steps, and fall down. Then I crawl back to the Cross and start all over again. I'm sick and tired of this rut. I want to go on. I want to keep walking. I need the infilling of the Holy Spirit. I want the same experience as the people in the Upper Room on the day of Pentecost.

Someone must have heard the desperation in my prayer and interjected some counsel, "Sister, all you need is to keep short accounts with the Lord. You don't need an ecstatic spiritual experience. You just need to confess your shortcomings daily, and you will be alright." Jesus, I don't want to be patronized. I want You. I need You. I need all You have to give. I can't live with anything less.

Lord, what is this? My eyes are closed, but I can see a long corridor in a church, just like the side aisle of my college church. The corridor is filled with golden light, and there is no end in sight. The light-filled corridor goes on and on. Somewhere in the sanctuary, a choir is singing, "Glory, glory, hallelujah. His truth is marching on."

Oh God, You heard my desperate cry and You answered. I will walk on forever down that golden corridor until I finally reach You face to face. I can walk in the light of Your truth. Your Spirit is truth, and it is marching on. Filled with Your Holy Spirit, I will be marching on! You are so good to me. The vision has faded, but the Truth remains. I know that I know that the Holy Spirit is coming to me, and I will have a consistent walk with You.

Days have passed since that beautiful vision, but I am still warmed by the message. You love me so much that You will provide the way for me to become Christ-like by giving me the Holy Spirit. Have I already received the Holy Spirit? There is a new joy inside. The Bible says in Luke 11:13 that my Father in heaven will give the Holy Spirit to those who ask him.

I asked; therefore, I must have received. But maybe not. Lord, there is so much I don't understand. Some people say that we receive the Holy Spirit at the moment of conversion. Others say that He comes when we ask for a "second blessing." Maybe they are both right. All I am really sure about is that I want all of You as I give You all of me.

And I really need all of You, because now I'm in the pits. All of the children have gotten the flu, including our six-month old baby. I am up day and night, cleaning up both ends of our little ones, and I'm panicked when I hear our baby cough.

What little sleep I do get is fitful, not renewing. I thought that after my great spiritual experience, life would be smoother. Why did You let this happen, God? Didn't You know I needed to deepen my spiritual disciplines with more time for scripture and meditation? I don't understand.

And here is my encouraging husband handing me the Bible to read before we fall exhausted into the bed. I groan, "I don't feel like reading the Bible." He responds in an equally spiritual tone, "I don't care if you want to or not. Just read it so we can go to sleep." Sassily I retort, "I suppose I'm going to open the Bible and God is going to speak directly to me."

A section of Romans 5 seems to be leaping off the page at me:

We also boast of our troubles, because we know that trouble produces endurance, endurance brings God's approval, and his approval creates hope. This hope does not disappoint us, for God has poured out his love into our hearts by means of the Holy Spirit, who is God's gift to us.

Romans 5:3-5 (GNT)

I am undone. The power of Your loving correction blended with encouragement has dissolved my resentment, leaving me melted in tears.

Then the realization hits me: You heard me. You know my name. You know where I live. You forgive me. Am I glad You don't hurl thunderbolts from heaven at sassy kids! I would be incinerated by now. You haven't turned Your back on me. Even in the midst of my complaining You still love me. Dancing about the room, I can't keep from exclaiming: "He hears me. He sees me. He loves me. He talks to me. Just maybe He really has gifted me with the Holy Spirit."

Life is better. I am learning to rejoice in my troubles, and the children are finally over the flu. But they are not ready to go outside on a day with such frigid temperatures. What do I do? David is going to make a quick trip across the alley to pick up some materials from the church, and the children are begging to go with Daddy, who says, "We won't be long. Just over and back. It will do them good to get out of the house."

"Well, okay, but be sure to tie their hoods tightly and put on their mittens."

"Mittens? We're only going across the alley."

"Put on their mittens," I firmly reply.

*Where are David and the kids? They've been gone a long time. David must have discovered an unfinished project. It's a good thing the children are bundled up well, because the church is not very warm during the week. Oh, here they come. It's about time. What is this? Snowsuits only partially zipped, hoods untied, and no mittens! The children's hands are ice-cold and I am hot! How did they get this cold in the church?*

"Well, they weren't in the church very long," was David's reply. "Since we were just running back across the alley, I didn't think we needed to bother with mittens and so on. I didn't count on being stopped in the alley by Larry Pritchard, our state patrolman, who needed to talk a little while. I guess it was longer than I thought."

I can feel my blood pressure rising. Isn't that just like a man? And who will have to get up in the night if they all get sick again? Not Daddy. But I won't make a scene. That would not become a newly Spirit-blessed wife.

Needless to say, our relationship has been a bit frosty during the remainder of the day. Very little has been said, except for my rather barbed remarks whenever David has done something that did not exactly please me—in fact, I haven't found much that pleased me all day. Finally the kids are asleep and we are sitting silently in front of our little TV set. David breaks the ice by saying, "I don't know what's wrong with me. I started the day feeling great. Now I feel lousy. I think I'll go to bed."

I don't even respond, but inside I'm thinking, *So you feel lousy? Serves you right. You've clicked off the TV and probably think I'm going to follow you upstairs to bed, but I'm not. I'm going to sit right here and stare at this blank screen. How could you forget to bundle up the children? How could you be so insensitive to my concerns?*

I guess I've stayed down here long enough to make my point. I can't stay up all night. Oh, no. David is waiting up for me and handing me the Bible. "Your turn to read." Opening to 2 Corinthians 2, I am riveted to verses ten and eleven: "When you forgive people for what they have done, I forgive them too. For when I forgive—if, indeed, I need to forgive anything—I do it in Christ's presence because of you, in order to keep Satan from getting the upper hand over us; for we know what his plans are" (GNT).

Stunned silence. I've been exposed. Oh, Lord, You are right. I didn't make a scene, but I nursed my anger and resentment all day long, wounding my husband and our relationship and letting our enemy divide us. I repent, Lord. David, I'm so sorry. Will you forgive me?

What an awesome realization: the God of the Universe is guiding us daily through His Word! I don't know how it happens, but specific directives from the Bible either get highlighted or magnified or something. All I know is that they stand out on the page, and the message zings right into my heart and mind.

We have so many markings and notations in this Bible that I hope we never lose it. It is a record of Your personal instruction just to us, Lord. You are a marvelous teacher. You certainly don't pull any punches. I seem to get nailed every time I open the Bible.

Ever since Your promise of the Holy Spirit in that vision, the Bible has come alive, and we are devouring, digesting, and allowing it to reshape our lives. No longer do I harbor hurt feelings, brooding and becoming depressed—in fact, the depression seems to be lifting. We quickly forgive each other, with Your help, of course. That passage in 2 Corinthians on forgiveness reprogrammed our responses big-time.

Even more exciting is our application of Ephesians 4:2-3 (GNT): "Be always humble, gentle, and patient. Show your love by being tolerant with one another. Do your best to preserve the unity which the Spirit gives by means of the peace that binds you together." Without a chip on my shoulder, I am expecting the best responses from David, and I'm getting them. I don't know how that works, but it does.

When I expected a negative reaction, I must have projected antagonism and thus received just what I anticipated. Now that we have the goal of unity in the Spirit, we are much more willing to give each other the benefit of the doubt. Tension is leaving our relationship, and trust is growing. Now that that awful screaming genie has been chased back into the bottle and the cork secured, the whole household is happier.

That old saying that if Mama ain't happy, ain't nobody happy surely is true. It's amazing how the children pick up on my moods. The more nervous I became, the more the children acted out their anxiety. Now they are much more peaceful because instead of their mommy screaming, she's singing. I'm not perfect. Sometimes I still start a tirade but catch myself and apologize. It's great to be able to tell myself to stop and to have my emotions obey.

Thank You for changing the atmosphere in our home by changing my heart attitudes. I used to sing, "Into my heart, come into my heart, Lord Jesus." Then I wondered as a child how that could be. If, as scientists say, my heart is no bigger than my fist, I thought You might be a little crowded between my liver and my spleen. Thank You for answering that quandary during my devotions.

You said, "I'm not living in your physical heart. I am living in your spirit. Your spiritual house is much larger than your physical house. Just as you draw strength from your husband's presence in the home, learn to draw strength from my presence in your spirit. When David is there to reinforce your discipline, you speak with more authority. Well, I'm always at home with you. Draw from that strength.

"I am closer than you think. Remember reading the account of an insecure choir member learning to sing with confidence? The lead tenor convinced him to lean into his chest, allowing the sound to resonate through him. I am here to sing through you. Lean into Me. I will fill you with My song and My Word. You will speak with My authority, My wisdom, and My compassion. Let Me live through you to change the atmosphere in your home and in your world." Thank You, Lord, for clarifying profound truth through simple explanations. Thank You for transforming me and my home.

# CHAPTER 7

# Free to Choose What God Chooses

We're on our way home from a counseling session, Lord, and I'm struggling. I wanted an appointment with Dr. Williams to help me sort out some relationship problems, and I also wanted to share some of my recent experiences of Your leading us. Now I am pondering his response: "Who calls the shots in your life?"

"I guess I would have to say that God does," I replied.

"That's a cop-out," he quickly retorted. "You have a free will. You are the one who makes the decisions."

I guess I didn't know how to reply and must have passively agreed.

Now on the way home with David, thoughts race through my mind. Life has been so much better since we've let You, Lord, direct us through the scriptures.

But Dr. Williams does have a point. I do have a free will, and I have to make choices. Yes, that's it! I do make choices but now I choose to choose what You choose.

You've given me a second chance at Eden. I don't want to bite into that bad apple of rebelling against Your sovereign decisions. I don't want to decide for myself what is good and what is bad. I don't want to be a rebellious adolescent who dares to taste the evil to decide if it really will kill me and then find myself poisoned. I want to choose what an all-knowing, all-loving parent sets before me and to trust that because You do love me, You set boundaries only to protect me.

I love You, Lord. I'm so glad the bottom fell out of my basket and I landed in a bog of depression. If everything had gone smoothly without any struggles, I probably would not have so doggedly sought You. Yes, people do find God in the crises of life. Thank You, Lord, for my crises. Thank You for putting me in the uncomfortable roles of pastor's wife and mother of three babies in three years. You certainly know how to encourage me to cry, "Help!"

You've certainly been our helper in the two churches You have called David to shepherd. We've begun to share our experience with people, and others are getting excited about hearing from You, Lord. Thank You for the new prayer group and new programs underway in our two little churches. Thank You for intervening in our church after David's desperate prayer.

He was at the end of his resources when he prayed, "God, I've done all I can do to pump new life into this church. I can't do it anymore. Nothing is going to happen unless You do it." I guess You've been waiting for that surrender so that You could take the reins.

Lord, we should have surrendered long ago. Ministry with David has become exciting. The church is no longer my rival, but an opportunity for sharing Your amazing love. It is thrilling to see You touch lives. People have come forward for salvation and rededication. Even the youth are getting involved. David finally convinced the trustees to open the church basement on Friday nights for a youth center. I especially enjoy the prayer group, where people are beginning to journal their own journey with You. Thank You.

Oh, no! It's time in the United Methodist Conference calendar for new appointments. We jokingly call this the time of Methodist musical chairs, but this is no joke for us this year. The district superintendent has just asked David to consider moving. David went through a whole litany of reasons for staying in this parish, but the superintendent persisted, asking David to pray about the possibility. He couldn't very well refuse that request. Now we need to hear from You, Lord.

It's late at night, and David has to give an answer about a move tomorrow. "Well, Lord," we pray, "Please give us an answer in the Scripture." Reading from Good News for Modern Man, David looks visibly shaken as he reads Romans 15:2-3: "My work in these regions is done."

My heart sinks. "Lord, You wouldn't take us far away from our parents. With three little ones, I depend on their help occasionally. Our parents are within easy driving distance. Please, Lord, I don't want to leave this place."

David quickly asks for another scripture. Acts 7 captures his attention. Verse 3 says in part: "Leave your family and country and go to the land that I will show you" (GNT). Turning to another passage, he reads one word. "Go." Through tears and with heavy hearts, we hold each other and surrender to Your plan.

Surrender can be risky. The wheels have been set in motion, and we don't like where the wagon may be taking us. The conference cabinet has accepted David's agreement to move, our two little churches have been notified that we are leaving, and we are facing an appointment that David doesn't want to take.

Of all the senior pastors in the conference, there is only one with whom he has had a negative experience. Now the cabinet is asking him to serve as an assistant to this pastor. We're stuck. But how can we go forward?

David's spirit could be crushed, along with his passion for ministry, in this difficult relationship. Nevertheless, You said to move. Our future is in Your hands. We've decided not to balk at getting into the wagon.

After surrendering a second time, we are being blessed by a seemingly divine intervention from You, Lord. A new position at the Wesley Foundation on Ball State University's campus has just been funded at the last minute. David has been chosen to fill that spot. Hurray! David loves the university setting, and so do I. In fact, I had counted on his career in higher education so that I could be a perpetual student.

And this university is home—eight miles from where I grew up. Although we didn't attend there, we both had been involved there. David had taken bassoon lessons from a Ball State professor and had played with him in the Muncie Symphony Orchestra. I had taken voice lessons on campus and been a part of the summer theatre program.

A special treat for me is that Dr. and Mrs. Ed Strother are there. As my high school English teacher, Mrs. Strother, had ignited a passion for learning in me and had encouraged me to excel. Dr. Strother, Chairman of the Drama Department, had graciously cast me in some good roles in the summer theatre.

In addition to all of these blessings is a beautiful gift: our parents in nearby communities. Once we surrendered our grasp on them, You have given them back to us. You knew all of this before we even said yes to a move. I'm glad we didn't resist.

Surrender and surprise must be related. When we've given up our will and our reasoning, You have been blessing us with more surprises. Your biggest surprise, which is an answer to my prayers, is the Spirit-filled fellowship that meets in David's cousin's home right here in town. I am excited.

These are lovely, gracious people. After visiting with them, we have come away with copious literature explaining the work of the Holy Spirit. You know that both of us have already asked for an encounter with the Holy Spirit, and we have been enjoying His ministry through the Scriptures and prayer, but we know there is more.

There are times when I need to express my love and gratitude for all that You have done for us, but even after singing all of my favorite hymns and choruses, I feel limited. My language is inadequate to express the deep emotion that yearns to be released. I think I need a heavenly language, but I don't know how to experience it. Unbeknownst to me, David, too, has been seeking. He had even been stopping by the Pentecostal Church in a nearby city during our last appointment, but he never found anyone available.

Maybe we needed time to overcome our fears and prejudices. We've never been in a Pentecostal service, and I'm a bit apprehensive. I might as well be honest. I've been a religious snob, looking down on what I considered store-front sects led by uneducated fanatics. Finding that the Pentecostal movement in the United States was actually started in 1900 by a Methodist pastor, Charles Parker, I felt somewhat reassured. I don't suppose that really makes any difference, but having a connection with something familiar has made me feel more comfortable.

But why should I need that reassurance? After all, Charles Parker was a Christian seeking what I am hungering for: an authentic encounter of the Holy Spirit as had been experienced in the Upper Room. Lord, maybe other people will consider me a fanatic also. That doesn't really matter anymore, because I have such a hunger for more of You that labels and reputations mean nothing in light of that desire. Please forgive me for being a religious and intellectual snob.

# CHAPTER 8

# Choosing the Holy Spirit

Lord, I surrender my lingering apprehensions about a heavenly language. I want one, but I guess I still have some fear, because I shrink back from even saying "speaking in tongues." That sounds strange. "Heavenly language" sounds more sedate and acceptable.

Then there seems to be some controversy about speaking in tongues. Some claim that this experience is a primary sign of receiving Your Holy Spirit, while others believe one can be filled with the Spirit without speaking in tongues. In 2 Corinthians 12:18, Paul suggests that not everyone speaks in tongues, just as not everyone is a prophet or a teacher.

But in 1 Corinthians 14:18, he thanks You that he speaks in tongues more than many others. This is all very confusing. All I'm sure about is that I want to be an effective follower of Yours, just like those in the New

Testament church, and I desire a spiritual language to communicate more deeply with You.

After reading John Sherrill's historical account of the Pentecostal movement and then our friends' literature on the Charismatic movement, I understand some basic truths that make me feel more secure. First, the Pentecostal movement, as well as the Charismatic movement, is Biblical.

Charles Parker and his band of seekers diligently studied the New Testament accounts of the ministry of the Holy Spirit and followed the Scriptures painstakingly. The offspring of the earlier Pentecostal movement, the charismatic movement, embraces the New Testament guidelines on operating in the gifts of the Holy Spirit.

Second, the evidence of changed lives and communities, plus numerous documented healings, both physical and emotional, testify to the validity of both movements. Jesus Himself called on the evidence of the miracles that He performed as proof of His divine mission (John 14:11). Likewise, the miraculous events documented in the Pentecostal and Charismatic movements testify to Your presence, Father, in their midst.

I may not fully comprehend everything about this new experience, but I have decided that the Baptism in the Holy Spirit and speaking in tongues is Biblical and valid for today. And I'm going for it. We're invited to the Friday night meeting at our friends' house. Please activate the faith I need to receive Your Spirit, Lord. In the case of receiving a prayer language, I guess I have to do the activating. That's what all of the instructions say, reminding me that You will give me what I ask for because You are a good Father.

I'm going to hang onto that thought. Then I must give You, Holy Spirit, my vocal cords and speak out whatever comes from You. David is going with me, but I'm not sure he is as rabid as I am about receiving a language. He's the real intellectual, Lord, and much more cautious and reserved. We are together in this thing though. Yes!

Oh my, this place is crowded! There are two seats fairly near the front, but we will have to crawl over several people to get to them. Well, Lord, the people look normal, even attractive. Oops! Forgive me for my prejudice. I'm not as open as I thought.

Someone in the back has started a chorus that I don't know, and everyone has joined in. Hope they sing something we know. I'll feel like a heathen, not knowing their customs and songs. I guess it doesn't matter. No one is looking at me anyway. They've all got their eyes closed. That's different. Their faces look radiant, as if they're seeing something. Maybe I should close my eyes, too. At last I hear a Gaither chorus I know. Now I can join in. This eye-closing thing is good. I can concentrate more on You, Lord.

What in the world is this? An angelic sound is rising and falling upon the air. No one seems to be directing, but the harmony and intonation are perfect. The sound rises and subsides, then rises again, all in unity. I'm afraid to open my eyes. I've either been transported to heaven, or angels have entered the room. Just one peek. No angels; just radiant upturned faces.

This must be the singing in the Spirit I've read about, Lord. I'd surely like to join this choir. As abruptly as it started, the anthem has finished. After a pregnant pause, someone speaks of Your love and approval, Lord, and of Your desire to bless Your children. I never heard anything like that in the United Methodist service. This surely is an adventure.

Oh. While I had my eyes closed, the speaker for the evening must have come to the front. He looks fairly normal, too. Just kidding, Lord. He's speaking on faith. Just what I need. He says we must follow the teaching in Mark 11:24 (KJV): "Therefore I say unto you, what things soever ye desire, when you pray, believe that ye receive them, and ye shall have them." He likes the King James Version, I see. Well, Lord, I'd better listen up. This message is for me.

Now he has finished speaking and is inviting anyone who wants to receive the Baptism in the Holy Spirit and the gift of speaking in tongues to come to the front for prayer. That's me. I'm getting up there right away. Whoa! David, who has been pinned in against the wall, is strong-arming me and going up ahead of me. I'm the one who has been bugging him to get in touch with his cousin and hounding him to take me to the meeting.

He's always polite and considerate of me. He must have gotten turned on. This is what I wanted, wasn't it, Lord? So why am I miffed at him? I'd better get in line, too. People around David are encouraging him and saying, "Keep speaking. You've got it." They're clapping and patting him on the back as if they're as happy as he is.

I hope I "get it" as easily. Just one person in front of me. I hope I'm ready. I feel shaky. My turn. The speaker is laying his hand on my forehead and saying, "Receive the Holy Spirit."

Suddenly I am blank. I don't know what to do. "Just speak whatever comes into your mind. Don't think about it. No. Don't pray in English. Let the Spirit have your vocal cords and your lips." I feel so conspicuous. What if I don't receive anything? David got it so easily. I'm supposed to be the emotive, spiritually hungry one.

This is so embarrassing. The only thing that comes to my mind is "Gallia O Mallia." That sounds so stupid. I'm not saying that. I must be making it up. You surely know how to humble me, Lord. I wish I had never come up here.

Everyone is speaking in their prayer language. Trying to prime my pump, I guess. Maybe I should just mimic what they're saying and escape. Everyone is waiting. "Gallia O'Mallia" is swelling and sticking in my throat. If I don't let it out, I may choke right here. Well, here goes. Now everyone is rejoicing. They say I've got it. I hope so. I'm as limp as a rag.

Lord, I want to trust you, but I thought I'd get a fluent language like what I've heard here tonight. I guess I'll have to trust and believe that You've blessed me with the Holy Spirit. The speaker must sense my frustration because he's saying that receiving has nothing to do with emotions. It is an act of my will to trust that what I ask for, You have given me.

Lord, You are so faithful. Even in my frustration of not immediately experiencing a prayer language, You kept me steady, as well as humbled, until I wanted You more than I wanted the gift. You kept bringing reassuring songs to my mind, and I found myself singing all day long.

And then it happened. I wasn't struggling or pouting. I was just praising You. I'm sure You were amused at my surprise while alone in the car the words of an old hymn changed into beautiful flowing syllables. I left the familiar tune and found myself singing a lovely melody in a language which I could not understand, but which released an overflowing well of joy.

In my excitement, I must not have realized that I was singing at the top of my lungs with the windows rolled down. Sitting at a stoplight, I became aware of the person in the car next to me staring at this strange woman. I lowered the volume but did not stop for fear that I might not be able to start again—in fact, I continued to sing until I burst through the front door singing at full volume. I stopped long enough to say, "I got it! I got it!" and started right where I left off. What a thrill to find that I could sing or pray in my new language whenever I chose. You are so good.

Jesus, I have never felt closer to You in all of my life. As a little girl, I longed to touch You as I stood on the hill under the bright stars. Now I believe that I do touch You through my prayer language. Every time I pray or sing in my new language, my spirit seems to soar into space where I make contact with You and then a shower of blessing travels back to me. It's a completed circuit of worship and praise and then blessing. I have tapped into an inexhaustible energy source. I am connected to You, the creator and sustainer of all things. Thank You.

I no longer have to wait for the next conference or camp to recharge my battery. If I stumble and slide into the valley of fear and self-condemnation, I can quickly ascend to the mountaintop where Your presence dwells through praising in my new language. In that place of intimacy I am forgiven and filled with love and confidence. Even if the circumstances do not change, I am changed and I can cope. Living on the mountaintop in the midst of the valley! That's awesome.

Knowing that You are as close as my very breath is even more awesome. Every morning I find myself slipping out of bed before the family awakens so that I can stretch my whole being to offer myself and my song to you. Then with tip-toe anticipation I await Your response, which thrills me to the core of my being.

Liquid love pours into my soul, healing the cracked and broken places caused by other people's criticism or insensitive remarks, and also by my own self-deprecation. Your love fills the empty spaces, and I no longer need to seek comfort in food or frenetic activity. I feel calm and at peace. I know who I am. I am Yours. I am loved.

Not only am I loved; I am free. Free and able to express thoughts and feelings that my conscious mind has not been able to acknowledge. After worshipping in my prayer language, I find myself speaking out thoughts that surprise me. I am acknowledging sins and shortcomings that I had never dared to admit.

Just the other day I was still smarting from what I perceived to be a betrayal. I tried to deny that I was angry, but after praying in my prayer language, I found myself blurting out my bitter hatred that had been buried under empty religious phrases of superficial piety.

I didn't fool You, Lord. You knew the buried bitterness, but You couldn't set me free from something that I refused to admit. In a different language I must have been confessing the real state of my heart. Then when I returned to English, the truth came out. What a relief to have that sore cleansed and healed.

Frustration at being controlled by people's opinions also welled up, and I spewed out years of pent-up anger. I named people whom I felt controlled me. Verbalizing my ugly resentment released a flood of emotion, as I wept uncontrollably. In the quiet that followed, I whispered prayers of forgiveness and experienced Your peace. A major boil had been lanced and drained of its poison.

You confirmed my freedom with a vision of me lying on a stone slab. I felt as if I were seeing myself in a morgue. As I looked at my dead body, I began to speak, "I am because You are, and whatever I become will be what You have made me." No longer does my identity depend on other peoples' opinions. I had died to the old identity of people-pleaser and then spoken my new identity in You. A friend pointed out that I had found a new lode star, giving me direction and purpose. Thank You, Lord, for the inner healing that is taking place in my life.

# CHAPTER 9

# Worship and Intercession

Perhaps the most healing experience that praying in my prayer language gives me is the abandonment I experience in worship. Thank You, Lord, for gifted teachers like Bob Mumford, who in his seminars encouraged me to cast aside all inhibitions about worshipping You. To find complete release in our prayer languages, he suggested getting alone and doing whatever we felt prompted to do by Your Holy Spirit, whether it was lying prostrate or dancing, singing or speaking. I took his advice and stayed back in the cabin while others at the camp went to their morning devotional groups.

After asking the Holy Spirit to guide me, I began to pour out my soul to You through my prayer language. The song started softly and slowly and I let my body follow the melody in smooth, flowing movements. As joy began to cascade over me, I started to dance with abandon and laugh uninhibitedly.

Anxieties and heaviness melted away. I was a child again, Your child. I was transparent, unaffected, vulnerable. Praying in my prayer language had opened deep recesses in my soul, and the feelings I could not release through singing in English came pouring out. I knew I had tapped into a spring of love that could finally be expressed.

After a while, my jubilant song subsided as tears of gratitude washed away all traces of reticence and unworthiness. Freely I poured out my love for You in soaring melodies that lifted my spirit into a heavenly realm. My whole being was reaching and longing for You. You did not ignore my overtures. Sensing Your presence, I knelt and then lay prostrate before You, absorbing Your love and peace. I finally left that little tabernacle, poured out and filled to overflowing.

Jesus, why would anyone scorn such a beautiful gift of heavenly communication? Yes, I know I had been skeptical, perhaps fearful, of what was an unfamiliar expression, but now I wish I had been blessed with a heavenly language from the very first encounter with You. Surely, I would have walked more consistently with You and have been less vulnerable to doubt. I know I would not have had to wait for a mountaintop experience at a camp or conference.

Through praising You, especially in my unhindered prayer language, I could have gone up the mountain any time I chose, just as I do now. I will never be a victim no matter what happens to me as long as I remember to praise You. Neither will I be a prisoner of my fluctuating emotions. I can choose to praise and thus release my spirit to take charge. I am free, free of plaguing fears and doubts. I am in touch with You and I know that You love me.

Jesus, You have freed me to know You through praise and worship, and that has changed my life and the life of my family. Now You are asking me to use this access and the new tools in prayer for others who are facing great trials. I pray that I am ready for this challenge.

I know You are ready. I recently proclaimed that I could be ready for any crisis through praising. But right now my spirit is so heavy with sorrow for my friends. You know them. They're Your kids, but the enemy has ambushed them. Their marriage is about to dissolve because the spirit of homosexuality has deceived and imprisoned the husband.

Counselors have advised the wife to get out of the marriage, taking their toddler with her, because they believe the husband will never be able to change his sexual orientation. After a lifetime of rejection from his father and many years of secretly finding acceptance in homosexual relationships, he appears to be forever trapped and incapable of fidelity to a heterosexual marriage. I keep trying to praise You in this situation, but my spirit is still heavy.

For days I have agonized in prayer without a sense of breakthrough. It's 3:00 a.m. and my spirit is troubled. If I can't sing in my prayer language, I'll just pray. Hopefully Your Spirit will reveal a new strategy to help my friends. I have cried all of my tears. I have nothing more to give. Holy Spirit, I need You to intercede through me. I have heard people talk of the groaning of the Spirit, but I have never experienced it.

My, this is different. I cannot speak in my normal prayer language. These words sound very guttural, very Germanic, very intense. And they have dredged up deep emotions that seem to wrench my whole being through wails and groans of pain. I thought I had cried all of my tears.

This new language has released a flood, and I can't control the sobbing. Now my words must be shouting commands. I seem to be attacking a wall. Even my body is lunging and pushing with every assaulting sentence. It's as if I have a drill in my hands and I am pressing with all of my might.

This process has gone on for a long time now. With one last gasp, the drill breaks through. There is no more resistance. Hallelujah! Yes, Yes, Yes. Holy Spirit, You did it! You did it! I don't know what You did, but You did it! Hurray! After all of those tears and wailings, I can't stop laughing. I hope I don't wake the family. If anyone has been awake, they must think I have lost it. But I haven't. I've found it! I've found a new prayer tool.

Months have passed since my night of intercession for our friends and I know that You, Lord, did win a battle through the Holy Spirit. You must grieve that the marriage did not survive, but You rescued the husband from a life of confusion and bondage and pain. Thank You for allowing us to participate in his freedom and restoration. I am most grateful for a supportive prayer community that also ministered to him. Now he is telling others that they, too, can be free.

Prayer is powerful. Praying in a heavenly language under Your Holy Spirit's direction is truly strategic warfare, pinpointing problems that I have no knowledge about in my natural understanding. How exciting to wake up hearing myself praying in tongues and then to slip out of bed to continue the adventure. Thank you, Lord, for telling me what has been happening.

Just the other day I had that experience, and You whispered to me that the prayer was for my mother. When I checked with her later in the day, she confirmed that she had been having a persistent pain. Before going to bed, she had decided that if the pain had not subsided by the next morning, she was going to go to the doctor. Upon awakening, she was relieved that the pain was gone, and it has not come back. I think You like to encourage me, Lord, so that I will keep praying.

Sometimes I get so excited about my new walk with You that I relate prayer experiences with others who cannot accept the validity of what I share and try to redirect my thinking. But I know that my prayers are directed by You, and the opinions of others do not sway me. I was particularly thrilled to awaken praying in tongues the other day and to know that You used me to bring about a new birth for someone.

Shutting myself up in the kitchen, I continued to pray and experienced the throes of childbirth. After laboring for a period of time, I felt a thrusting forth and knew that the intercession had brought forth life. Thank You for reassuring me by whispering, "A new name has been written in the Lamb's Book of Life." I don't know who it was, but it doesn't matter. I was humbled to be included in Your grand scheme of life and redemption. What a privilege!

Later, as I reflected on the awesome responsibility and privilege of intercession, I remembered a friend in a speech and drama department trying to convince me that my new understanding of Christianity was too simplistic and very naïve. At home alone My spirit rose up and said, "No, that is not true. Life in the Holy Spirit is art in its highest form. In intercessory prayer I get to be a player in the cosmic drama of good triumphing over evil. No Greek comedy or tragedy could be as profound."

I have always loved the theater and enjoyed my brief time on the stage in college and in summer theater at the university near my home. Now I often find myself acting out the intercession, sometimes imaginatively holding a troubled girl in my arms and gently stroking her long hair as I pray softly in tongues. At other times I march back and forth, shouting commands as I engage in spiritual warfare.

While praying for a dear friend on the telephone, I found myself speaking in tongues with great authority and using my arms as a machete, whacking away at something like a thick hedge of interlocked brambles. As a result of this prayer time, my friend experienced a release from a place of bondage which had held her a prisoner. The spiritual prayer comes first, and then my body follows the flow of language, confirming the event taking place in the spiritual realm.

Thank You, Lord, for assuring me that my physical gestures are not contrived but Holy Spirit inspired. I keep hearing the song that speaks of singing when the Spirit says, "Sing," of dancing when the Spirit says, "Dance." I remember the day when You revealed to me that the Holy Spirit is my heavenly conductor, directing which art form would be pleasing to You each day.

I recall asking, "Heavenly conductor, how shall we worship the Father today? Shall we sing or shall we dance? Shall we wait in silence? Lead me. Use me as an instrument of worship." On a daily basis You never disappoint me, Holy Spirit. You always give me fresh inspiration that ushers me into communion with Your triune presence.

I can never forget the day that You revealed the beauty of interactive prayer. David and I had just attended a marriage seminar in which the speaker commented on his ability to spot the couples in any audience because the pair moved in harmony with each other even while seated. He noted that as one partner would shift positions, the other partner would respond with a corresponding movement.

Later, in morning worship, You reminded me of that lecture and spoke to me saying, "In prayer you are my partner in a heavenly ballet. I begin a movement, an inspiration, in heaven and, reaching down, I touch you, my partner. Then in response, you complete the movement on earth by praying My will into being." Dancing with my creator—moving in harmony through life's ups and downs. What a privilege. Yes, Spirit-led prayer is art at its highest form—creativity for Eternity.

# CHAPTER 10

# Restoration

Being Your partner is far removed from being Your pouting, doubting accuser. You have been so good to me. I remember those dark days when I cried from my pit of depression, "Are You up there? Do You hear me? Do You care? Do You have a plan?" You certainly did have a plan, and You executed it patiently and consistently. You never gave up on me. That's why I like the beginning of Psalm 40 so much:

> I waited patiently for the Lord;
>     He turned to me and heard my cry.
> He lifted me out of the slimy pit,
>     Out of the mud and mire;
> He set my feet on a rock
>     And gave me a firm place to stand.
> He put a new song in my mouth,
>     A hymn of praise to our God.
>                     Psalm 40:1-3a (NIV)

I didn't consistently wait patiently, but You did hear me, and You lifted me out of my pit and caused me to walk on a firm path steadily. And You gave me a new song of praise. Those statements encapsulate Your rescue operation for me. It sounds so simple, but in that simple plan there have been multiple complexities and setbacks. Certainly the transformation didn't happen overnight—in fact, the operation is still in progress. I am still a fallible human being in a fallen world, and I am constantly in need of a compassionate, persistent Savior.

Compassionate, persistent, and wise Savior. Lord, that is who You have been to me. First, in Your infinite wisdom You allowed me to fall into the pit, knowing that without desperation in my life I would not have reached for You with all of my being. As an unwise parent, I sometimes tried to keep our children from struggles without realizing that I was hindering their growth.

Underneath my genuine concern for them was the selfish truth that I didn't want to have to endure the pain of having children in pain. In contrast to my selfish motivation, Your infinite love compelled You to let me exercise my own free will and then experience my pain with me.

Love equipped You to reach for me in spite of the slime, muck, and mire in my pit. Love allowed You to risk the rejection and resistance emanating from my woundedness. Love absorbed my railings and accusations, my pouting and sulking. Holding me in Your embrace, You melted my resistance into surrender and readiness for recreation.

The books, the people, and the conference experiences You brought across my path gave me hope that there was something more to reach for. Then You gave me the humility and courage to reach and the grace to receive a renewed relationship with You as Savior and giver of the Holy Spirit.

Your Spirit revealed treasures in Your Scriptures and showed me how to apply them to my life. You placed me in a loving fellowship of believers, where I received teaching and mentoring in praise and worship and the study of Your Word. In private and corporate fellowship with You I learned to hear Your voice and walk in Your ways. Then You taught me to rest in You through believing faith. After all of this preparation, You revealed Yourself as Father, and I entered into the security and fellowship of my eternal family, the triune God.

One morning You revealed the overall picture of Your presence and Your work in me. In worship I became aware of Your infinite, multifaceted nature. A warm blanket of love settled over me, and I knew that You, Father, had the master plan for my life. You knew I would be overwhelmed and stumble, and You sent Jesus to save me.

Then Jesus sent the Holy Spirit to lead and guide me. And finally Jesus ushered me into Your presence. The awareness of Your loving care enveloped me in heavenly warmth. I heard myself saying, "Jesus, You bought me; then You sought me, through the Holy Spirit You taught me; and finally You brought me to the Father."

This summary of Your restoration process sounds so lofty and almost unattainable, but in the trenches of everyday life each step was gutsy and real to me. I came into the fellowship of Spirit-filled believers walking, but walking with a limp, strengthened but still weak in many areas. You graciously gave me two trusted mentors who never condemned me but identified with me and pointed me to a deeper place in You.

I remember calling Betty Klem and saying, "Betty, the kids are driving me up the wall and I'm about to lose control." She empathetically said, "Joyce, I know just what you're going through. John used to come home to find me sitting on the floor crying while Kathy and Johnny ran wildly about tearing up the house. After praying with John, I could focus on Jesus and find the strength to get up and take charge again. The more I talked to Jesus, the stronger I got. So I just talked to

Him all day long, and I forgot to feel sorry for myself or to allow my inadequacies to paralyze me."

The more she talked about You, the more confident and outward-focused I became. Later I realized what a gift she had given me. She didn't berate me for my spiritual weakness and tell me to take two quick Scriptures and call her in the morning. Instead, she walked back into the swamp with me, identified with my dilemma, and, riveting my gaze on You, walked out of the bog with me.

Emma Mitchell showed me how to continue in close fellowship with You. She said that whenever she felt estranged from You, she would quickly examine what had happened just prior to her inability to worship freely. Then she could repent and be restored. Both women modeled praise, worship, applying the Scriptures to all life experiences, and fervent intercession for others. Betty and Emma were my "Jesus with skin on."

Following their example, I committed myself to a consistent devotional life of praise and worship and pouring over the Scriptures. Without the support of my caring husband, I probably would not have had the willpower to keep that commitment. By this time, You had blessed us with another beautiful daughter. Knowing my limited time and energy level, David mercifully rearranged his schedule so that he could take the three older children on outings in the mornings.

As soon as our little Julie was down for her morning nap, David would leave with her brother and two sisters, and I would grab my Bible and begin to sing the Psalms or favorite hymns and choruses or new songs in my prayer language. Singing, praying, and reading became so intertwined that I couldn't seem to analyze which was helping me the most. The more I worshipped, the more understanding I received from Your Word; and the more I understood about You from Scripture, the more I worshipped.

Later, through Judson Cornwall's *Let Us Draw Near*, a study of the tabernacle, I began to understand the relationship of praise, Scripture, and worship in communing with You. In the arrangement of the appointments in the Holy Place, Cornwall demonstrated the correspondence of the Old Testament worship experience to what we enter into through You in our day.

"The Lampstand," or the "Revelation Light of the Holy Spirit," shines with great illumination on the Shewbread, which is Jesus, our bread of life, the Word. The Altar of Incense before the curtain of the Holy of Holies is the place of our offering of the "sacrifice of praise." When that sacrifice is accepted, we gain entrance into the Holy of Holies, where You dwell, offering mercy and communion.

Worship leaders in Women's Aglow Fellowship further taught me to wait before the Holy of Holies following the sacrifice of praise. After the sacrifice is accepted, You graciously reveal Yourself.

I know that the veil was rent in two at the point of Your completed sacrifice on the cross. The problem for me is the veil over my own eyes. My vision is blurred by clouds of self doubts, offenses I harbor, and misconceptions of You. I remember a teaching that You, Holy Spirit, are the one who carries out the commission to "pray without ceasing" in 1 Thessalonians 5:17 (KJV). Living within us, You become the needed cleansing agent bubbling in constant prayer, loosening the sludge of sin so that it can rise to the surface to be washed away.

Thank You for being my cleansing agent so that I can see more clearly. When I focus on You through praise, I am lifted out of preoccupation with self, and I really can come boldly before Your throne. Gazing on the true picture of You in the scriptures and songs that I sing in praise, I eagerly await the coming of my loving creator. But I am never fully prepared for the glimpse that You give me. Like many in Scripture, upon glimpsing a small portion of Your glory, I am undone, limp, and speechless.

I treasure the time You visited me during my study of Job. Nursing the festering sores of disappointments and unanswered questions, I agonized with Job. I too wanted to bring my complaints before You. Why did little Lynette die when so many had travailed in prayer for her recovery?

Her death left a despairing ache inside of me and opened the door to doubt and fear. What if I couldn't muster up enough faith to secure healing for one of my own children someday? I had been so sure You would answer my prayers the way I believed You would. With gusto, I had sung the Scripture in 1 John 5:14-15 (KJV):

> This is the confidence that we have in him,
> that, if we ask anything according to his will,
> he heareth us: And if we know that he hear
> us, whatsoever we ask, we know that we have
> the petitions that we desired of him.

I had the faith formula down pat, and I worked that formula daily, fully expecting that Lynette would rally from the coma to vindicate the efficacy of the prayers of many righteous men and women.

When she died, my faith did not completely die, but my understanding of the prayer of faith certainly needed to be put on life-support. As did Job, I wanted You to answer my questions: "Oh that I knew where I might find him! That I might come even to his seat! I would order my cause before him, and fill my mouth with arguments" (Job 23:3-4, KJV).

I could identify with Job's futile whining and flailing about in an effort to find You and force You to listen and answer. "Behold, I go forward, but he is not there; and backward, but I cannot perceive him: On the left hand, where he doth work, but I cannot behold him: he hideth himself on the right hand, that I cannot see him" (Job 23:8-9, KJV).

Like Job, I was the one who was lost in my own dust storm of doubts and demands. But suddenly You found me clutching my filthy rags of self-righteousness and arrogance. No longer was just Job on trial; I was the one exposed before the all-knowing, all-powerful creator of the universe. As You proclaimed Your sovereignty, Your majesty, wisdom and power, a weighty presence settled upon me.

In Job 40:8 (KJV), You hurled Your arrow into my puffed-up arrogance, and I was utterly humbled. "Wilt thou also disannul my judgment? Wilt thou condemn me, that thou mayest be righteous?" I sat powerless and paralyzed before You. I was speechless, but my heart cried out, acknowledging that You are God and I am not.

I wish I could say that I never again tried to assume Your role, especially in dealing with our children, but for that time I knew who You were and who I was. With humble gratefulness I could say with Job, "I have heard of thee by the hearing of the ear; but now mine eye seeth thee, Wherefore I abhor myself, and repent in dust and ashes" (Job 42:5-6, KJV).

For a long while I sat motionless, absorbing Your nearness. I had been corrected, but I was not abandoned; the rift in our relationship had been healed. Unanswered questions no longer held center stage in my soul. You were sovereign, and that is all the answer I needed. You loved me enough to correct me. Understanding would eventually come. I was at peace. With this new understanding, I determined to seek You even more diligently through continued praising, studying the Word, and worshipping Your presence.

# CHAPTER 11

# Sacrifice of Praise

Over the years, You expanded my understanding of the importance of praise and worship. I was set on fire by Bob Mumford's message, "The Sacrifice of Praise." At the Tennessee/Georgia Christian Camp, he taught us that the two Old Testament sacrifices that continued to be practiced in the New Testament church were the offering of first fruits and the fellowship offering. He reminded us of Peter's charge to believers to be "a holy priesthood, to offer up spiritual sacrifices, acceptable to God by Christ Jesus" (1 Peter 2:5, KJV).

Those acceptable sacrifices are verbal praises. "By him therefore let us offer the sacrifice of praise to God continually, that is, the fruit of our lips giving thanks to his name" (Hebrews 13:15, KJV). "I will therefore that men pray everywhere, lifting up hold hands, without wrath and doubting" (1 Timothy 2:8, KJV). "Let my prayer be set forth before thee as incense; and the lifting up of my hands as the evening sacrifice" (Psalm 141:2, KJV).

Mumford further pointed out that David had long ago perceived that the real sacrifice that God ultimately wanted was praise from the heart. "I will praise the name of God with a song, and will magnify him with thanksgiving. This also shall please the Lord better than an ox or bullock that hath horns and hoofs" (Psalm 69:30-31, KJV).

I learned from this teaching that sacrifice is not an onerous obligation to fulfill even though we don't feel like it. It is a joyous opportunity to enter into Your presence and also to invite Your presence into our situations. Psalm 22:3 says that You inhabit the praises of Your people. When You come on the scene, everything changes. Mumford asked and answered the loaded question: "What happened in the Old Testament when the sacrifice was accepted? The fire fell!"

As a Bible school student, Mumford used to go to the prayer chapel at 5:00 a.m. and fall asleep at 5:10 a.m. After he learned to offer the morning sacrifice, he experienced Your fire licking up his sacrifice and filling him with power to pray for everyone around the world and back.

Mumford's testimony enflamed me with a passion for praise and confirmed my earlier calling from You to be a singer in Your temple. In my Bible study I believe You kept bringing me back to passages in 1 Chronicles which spoke of the singers appointed by David "to stand every morning to thank and praise the Lord, and likewise at even" (1 Chronicles 23:5, KJV). David wanted songs of joy to fill the temple: "David told the leaders of the Levites to appoint their brothers as singers to sing joyful songs, accompanied by musical instruments: lyres, harps, and cymbals" (1 Chronicles 15:16, NIV).

Singing throughout the day came naturally for me, because I grew up hearing my sweet mother singing hymns as she did her household chores. The gift that she gave me became my offering to You. Joy began to fill my heart and our home. I underlined and memorized as many verses on joy and singing as I could.

My very favorite was Psalm 63:1-8. I made up a tune and sang it over and over. I could not sing it to You without tears welling up in my eyes. The Today's English Version seemed to capture the urgency and fervor that I felt within me:

> O God, you are my God,
> And I long for you.
> My whole being desires you;
> Like a dry, worn-out and waterless land,
> My soul is thirsty for you.
> Let me see you in the sanctuary;
> Let me see how mighty and glorious you are.

Your constant love is better than life itself,
And so I will praise you.
I will give you thanks as long as I live;
I will raise my hands to you in prayer.
My soul will feast and be satisfied,
And I will sing glad songs of praise to you.
As I lie in bed, I remember you;
All night long I think of you,
Because you have always been my help.
In the shadow of your wings I sing for joy.
I cling to you, and your hand keeps me safe.

Psalm 63 expressed my deep longing, seeking, reaching, feasting, praising, and meditating. But most of all, it painted a picture of me singing for joy under the shadow of Your wings.

Through this Psalm I realized my calling: singing for joy. And sing I did, morning, noon, and night and all of the times in between. Naturally my family didn't always appreciate all of the aspects of my singing. As teenagers, the kids sometimes complained, "Mom, you've sung that song a hundred times."

I learned to hum or to sing on the inside, but I hardly ever stopped singing. One day You showed me why. Slipping quietly into the living room at 5:00 a.m., I began to seek Your help in my devotional time. I had grand ideas of lofty worship, but all that would come were secular tunes. First I heard myself singing, "Without a song, the road would never bend; without a song a man ain't got a friend, without a song."

*That's not worshipful*, I thought and shut it off. Then I found myself singing "With a song in my heart heaven opens its portals to me." In frustration I cried out, "Lord, please give me something spiritual, something truly uplifting. I want a hymn of praise, not show tunes." When I heard myself singing "The hills are alive with the sound of music," I finally got it.

In a flash I was back in eighth-grade science class, completing an experiment of creating a vacuum in a tin can by boiling out all of the water and steam. Upon removing the can from the pan of boiling water, it collapsed under the force of gravity.

Instantly I understood what You were saying. I can still hear the words You spoke to me: "If you don't keep your soul buoyed up with the breath of the Spirit through songs of praise, the cares of this life will squash you flat." This was a sobering message, full of hope and warning at the same time.

Later I understood the implications of the warning. You always bring the right truth at the right time. In *Destined for the Throne* by Paul Billheimer, I found a profound explanation of the power of praise. First, praise brings mental and emotional health through shifting our focus from self to You, our all-knowing, all powerful, all-loving God Who wants only the best for Your children.

Knowing Your character through praise accompanied with study of scripture gives us confidence that Romans 8:28 (KJV) is true: "For we know that all things work together for good for those who are called according to his purpose." Thus praise frees us from the tyranny of self-preoccupation.

In a lecture on mental and emotional health, I had learned that a healthy person is generally outward focused, but an unhealthy person is primarily inward focused, resulting in various maladjustments—the worst of which is complete withdrawal into the catatonic state. E. Stanley Jones states in *Victory Through Surrender* that "when self becomes the center, becomes God, devastation reigns—and there are no exceptions."[2] He goes on to quote a head of a mental institution, saying of the residents, "they don't think of a thing except themselves. They are pickled in themselves. That's why they are here."[3]

You knew that I needed to get outside myself, and Your encouragement pushed me out of my comfort zone to a place where I had to rely totally on You. When the president of the local chapter of Women's Aglow Fellowship asked me to become the next worship leader, I froze in fear. I wasn't a musician; I just liked to sing. My husband was the musician. I couldn't read music well. I didn't have a good sense of pitch. My sister often complained that my pitch was flat when she tried to harmonize with me. Trying to compensate, I was accused of being too sharp.

When my husband tried to accompany my singing on the piano, he often had to scramble to find my key. I guess I often chose weird key signatures. I could follow the tune if played loudly on the piano, but leading was a scary proposition. Therefore, I protested, "Lord, I can't do that." You countered, "Yes, I know you can't, but I can." That settled that! At the next meeting, I stood in front of a sea of expectant faces, closed my eyes, and sang my heart out to You, and Your presence came. Humbled and awed, I whispered to You, "Yes, You can."

Soon after that, I attended an area training conference, during which the area director picked three worship leaders at random to lead a short worship time so that she could critique and instruct. I shriveled inside when she pointed to me. Thankfully she chose to delay the agony until the next morning.

Trying desperately to come up with songs that almost everyone knew and I felt confident enough to lead, I was about to be taken over with fear when I heard my spirit rise up. "Jesus, I feel like such an inexperienced novice and I feel so insignificant among these women that I do not know very well, but I know You and that's all that matters."

The next morning, shaking in my shoes, I opened my mouth and depended completely on You to use my vocal cords as You chose. You took the challenge and showed me that Your song could move people to tears and open them up to a time of healing, as many later shared. From then on, I fully expected You to sing through me to do Your work, and You never failed.

For several years I walked under the cloud of Your anointing to lead others into Your presence. If others complimented me on my skills in praise and worship, I was embarrassed, because I knew it had nothing to do with skill, but everything to do with relationship. You had rescued me from depression, and I couldn't stop thanking You. The intensity of my song emanated from my intimate times with You. You were my life, and I knew that without You I could easily slip back into darkness and defeat.

I was a desperate worshipper, and the more I worshipped, the more You revealed Yourself as the lover of my soul. In morning worship one day, a psalm began to bubble up in my spirit. Grabbing a pen, I wrote furiously as You inspired my worship to you:

> Shimmering through the mist, the sun announces the new day, pregnant with possibilities. Will He come soon? Is He anticipating my song? Has He heard the beating of my

heart? The mourning dove's soft coo awakens a melody within my soul and the clear call of the cardinal ignites my song. Softly rising and falling, the tune is lifted by the early morning breeze. The air vibrates with the presence and I am lifted out of the grasp of daily schedules and heavy burdens. A window has opened in my soul and I am released. My spirit reaches for You, my God. With the Psalmist I cry, "You, God, are my God, earnestly I seek you; I thirst for you, my whole being longs for you, in a dry and parched land where there is no water" (Psalm 63:1, NIV). Yes, "My soul and body crieth out, yea for the living God" (Psalm 84:2, KJV). The longing crescendos into a cry of ecstasy. My Lord, my Love, You are here. Your beauty overwhelms me. I fall at Your feet, gasping, for You have taken away my breath. In the hushed silence I wait, anticipating Your nearness. The weight of Your glory annihilates any hint of resistance. I am Yours. Your spirit intertwines with my spirit. Your presence saturates my soul. There is no space for separation. I am one with my Lord. Suspended in timelessness, I am complete. Oh, that You would stay until the sun sets and then linger until the mist rises before the clarifying sun. Alas, I sense Your glory lifting, but I am not really alone. Your touch lingers in my soul. I rise to meet the new day, empowered by Your Spirit. I walk into the full sunlight carrying Your will and purpose within me. Oh, Lord, my God, my Love.

Often, I have pondered the time You visited me with the same weightiness as when You revealed Your majesty through the final chapters of Job. Again, I was powerless in Your presence. Wave after wave of intense love poured over me. I could not have escaped Your presence if I had tried. I could not even raise one little finger. I was transfixed.

At first, I was taken aback by Your thoughts filling my consciousness. You spoke in the most intimate terms of marriage. Overcoming my shock and shyness expressed by my audible gasp, You reassured me by whispering, "I am your spiritual husband. Trust Me in the purity of My love." Like Mary, I have pondered this experience in my heart, nourishing my love for You.

Some may accuse me of the height of arrogance to compare my visitation from You to that of the time of Your holy conception, but I am convinced that You desire to overshadow each one of us with Your Holy Spirit to bring about the indwelling life of Christ. You want to plant Your Holy Seed within us. In Colossians 1:27

(NIV), You revealed the great mystery hidden throughout the ages from many generations: "Christ in you, the hope of glory."

For years I tried to be like You and always failed miserably. I read Charles Sheldon's *In His Steps* and tried to walk in Your footsteps, but I experienced as much frustration as I did, trying to step into my daddy's footprints in the deep snow. My stride could never match his. Even if I did get one foot in his boot print, I would fall face down in the snowdrift trying to reach his next step.

Then the truth of Galatians 2:20 (KJV) penetrated my understanding. You were already within me. "I am crucified with Christ: nevertheless I live; yet not I, but Christ liveth in me, and the life which I now live in the flesh I live by the faith of the Son of God, who loved me and gave himself for me." You are living in me, not out there beyond my stride. You are walking in my boots, and I don't have to keep falling on my face trying to lunge for Your footsteps. Hallelujah!

Even with this new understanding, I needed to let Your life mature within me. You had already been facilitating that process, and You revealed the scope of it during a time of puzzlement. I had been carefully taught by Bob Mumford about the wonders of the sacrifice of praise, but I didn't grasp the full import of it yet.

I had rejoiced in being Your priest, bringing sacrifices to You, until I began to be troubled over the word "sacrifice." Flashbacks of old movies depicting the pagan sacrifice of beautiful maidens to appease the gods of the volcanoes and even the superstitions of leaving food on the doorstep to pacify and ward off evil spirits bothered me greatly.

I began to question why You would even want us to be involved in something that smacked of paganism. Of course, in my questioning, I was not acknowledging the corruption by evil men and evil spirits of Your necessary institution for the saving of mankind. I was just repulsed by the thought of "feeding the gods" in pagan cultures, never knowing if the offering would satisfy their capricious natures. For a time, I even had trouble worshipping freely.

Then You brought insight. A friend of mine, Irma Cunningham, shared a dream that had disturbed her. She saw the baby Jesus lying in bed beside her infant son. She was awed that the baby Jesus would be in her house, and in her dream she felt too afraid to approach him; therefore, she fed only her son and avoided getting too close to the divine baby. As a result, her son grew to maturity, but the baby Jesus remained a helpless baby.

I was thinking about that dream when I read a wonderful devotional writing speaking of the necessity to mature in our relationship with You. The writer said that we could either nurture the life of Jesus, or we could ignore that life and remain stunted and immature.

Immediately I knew the interpretation of Irma's dream. She needed to overcome her fear of getting too close to Jesus and to nurture His life so that He could come to fullness within her. No longer did the idea of "feeding" Jesus bother me. I was simply nurturing Your growth inside of me, not leaving food at the doorstep of a pagan temple.

I could resume my offering the sacrifice of praise, knowing that I was participating in Galatians 2:20 (KJV): "I am crucified with Christ; nevertheless I live; yet not I, but Christ liveth in me." How clever You have been in causing me to seek understanding and then providing new insights.

Being a thorough teacher, You continued to hammer home the truth of Your living within me. I became fascinated with Your multiplying the loaves of bread to feed the multitudes and then revealing to the people that You are the bread of life. Through the sacrifice of praise and absorbing Your Word, I had been feeding You, and You had been feeding me. Our lives were being intertwined until I could be a part of Your prayer to the Father in the book of John.

My prayer is not for them alone. I pray also for those who will believe in me through their message; that all of them may be one, Father, just as you are in me and I am in you. May they also be in us so that the world may believe that you have sent me.  I have given them the glory that you gave me, that they may be one as we are one; I in them and you in me. May they be brought to complete unity to let the world know that you sent me and have loved them even as you have loved me.

John 17:20-23 (NIV)

# CHAPTER 12

# Inner Healing

Sometimes we are so full of ourselves and our problems that we haven't left room for You. No doubt that's why You started sweeping out the debris in my spiritual house. Actually, the process felt more like a cleansing fire than a gentle broom.

I remember wondering what was coming when a Bible study leader prayed for me and said she could see a cauldron full of molten metal. Periodically the fire underneath would increase, and rising to the top was the dross that was being skimmed off by a large ladle. Then the fire would subside, only to increase again with the same skimming process.

She interpreted this vision to mean that You were starting a process of purification that would extend over a period of time until all of the dross was removed, leaving a purified precious metal. In the refining of silver, the process is complete when the artisan can see his own reflection in the liquid.

She encouraged me to endure the refining so that Your image could be seen in my life. I knew there were dark places of hurt, jealousy, and resentment that marred Your reflection in me; therefore, I submitted to the process.

In the next few months, You proved Yourself to be the best, most thorough counselor that ever existed. You delved deep within my soul, cleansing and healing to release me into great joy and freedom. From time to time, You would begin to trouble me about a sin in my life that I had covered over with excuses but had not really dealt with. I could not get peace until I acknowledged my thoughts or behaviors as sin and let You lift them out of my life. Sometimes You made me confess my sin to others, even if a long time had passed, and I thought it unnecessary to bring it up.

When You began to trouble me with the issue of truth and honesty, You even made me write to a high school teacher to confess that I had changed an answer on a returned test, not knowing that the scores had not yet been recorded. When he asked for the papers back to enter the grades in his book, I did not tell him I had corrected an answer. It bothered me for a while, but as time went on, I forgot about it.

You did not forget. I could not get away from Psalm 51, especially verse 6a: "Behold, thou desirest truth in the inward parts" (KJV). Writing that excruciatingly painful letter convinced me that any form of lying or deceit was not worth the price of painful confession. But the peace and self-respect I experienced were certainly worth it.

Much of the healing had to do with old wounds deep within that I had mostly forgotten until You allowed circumstances to bring them to the surface. I came to describe them as puss pockets that erupted when someone, usually my husband, happened to bump into them.

Forgiveness was always the key for healing. Remembering how Jesus had held his peace when tormented, I wondered why He didn't retaliate? Surely there were plenty of wounds to cause painful places inside His soul. My husband reminded me that Jesus immediately forgave, preventing festering infection.

We had already learned the power of forgiveness through the healing ministries of Agnes Sanford and Anne White. David had attended training sessions on "inner healing" and had brought home books and recordings. I began to contemplate the nuances of forgiveness, particularly the three-fold steps taught by Anne White.

The first step requires forgiving the offender. The second step is asking the Lord to forgive the person. The last step, which really caught my attention, is to ask God for forgiveness for harboring the offense, allowing a root of bitterness to grow.

I didn't know how soon I was going to have to put that three-step plan into practice. You always put together the pieces of the puzzle at just the right time. Without my realizing it, You were again fanning the flames for my purification and healing.

This particular fire began to heat up in the dead of winter. In mid-January my husband was preparing for a winter retreat with the Wesley Foundation students at Ball State University, leaving me at home in the country with four little ones.

Priding myself as being the dedicated, supportive wife, I began collecting my husband's winter gear and packing his warmest clothes, but somewhere in the process I stopped thinking about serving my husband and began thinking about being left alone with the kids while he was reveling in winter sports and having great fellowship.

The more I pondered my plight, the less caring and supportive I felt. Actually, I didn't feel supportive at all. I was becoming angrier by the minute. By the time David had put his belongings in the car and was saying his final good-byes, I was near an explosion point. His parting comment was the match that set me off: "I really hate to go. This is going to be an exhausting weekend."

Kerboom! All of my resolve to be a supportive wife went up in smoke, and I let out a volley of words that shocked us both: "My poor dear, you're going to have to sled down the hills and skate on the ice and drink that nasty hot chocolate. After that, you'll have to play endless games of ping-pong and then sing to the guitar around the roaring fire in the lodge. Such hard work! I feel so sorry for you."

Turning my back on my stunned husband, I left the room. With no warm embrace or encouraging prayer, he left the house. As he pulled out of the driveway, I was overcome with remorse. "What on earth compelled me to act that way? I never talk to David like that. If I were he, I wouldn't want to come home to a witch like that. Oh, God, help us."

All weekend as I met the many needs of the children, I kept repenting and asking for Your understanding of my anger. Alone in the darkened living room one evening, I received Your answer through a vivid memory. Suddenly I was back at the very campground where my husband was probably sitting by the fire, but in this memory it was a hot summer day during senior high youth camp.

David was shepherding our young people along with the group from a neighboring church in a crowded rustic cabin. By mid-week, tensions and tempers were escalating and threatening the peace of this supposedly idyllic setting. The two youth groups were not communicating well, and the two cooks, one from each church, were feuding. Adding to this stress was a suicidal girl from a different church background who couldn't relate to the denominational presentation of the week's message.

Needless to say, my husband, the young shepherd, already had almost more than he could handle. Rationally I could understand why he didn't have time for me, but emotionally I was wounded and deeply disappointed. More than at any time in our marriage, I desperately needed his support and comfort.

Just one day before his leaving for youth camp, we had suffered a devastating loss. After months of infertility treatments, I had finally conceived. We had spent hours planning for our expected new arrival and pouring over the motherhood book to check out our little one's progress from just a speck to a few inches.

Then came the miscarriage on the Saturday before my husband had to preach on Sunday morning and leave with our youth group for a weeklong camp. There was no time to mourn, only time to finish sermon preparations and pack.

Reluctantly, David left me behind to recuperate. In the middle of the week when friends from seminary days stopped through our little town, I eagerly accepted their invitation to visit David at the camp. Since I was feeling better, I decided to spend the remainder of the week with my husband. I envisioned strolling along the lake near the spot where we had spent our honeymoon and finding solace in each other's presence.

Instead, I walked the campgrounds by myself, nursing my hurt feelings and longing for my husband's attention. It was a former pastor who counseled and comforted me. I kept telling myself that David didn't intend to turn away from me. He probably just had to put the whole situation on hold and expected me to do the same; nevertheless, I was surprised at his seeming indifference to our loss.

When we returned home, he apologized for not having the emotional energy to meet my needs, and I dutifully forgave him and apologized for adding undue stress to his week. We quickly put the matter behind us as we finished the summer church assignment and prepared for a move to Massachusetts for David's graduate work.

Within a few months we were expecting again. We joyfully welcomed our beautiful daughter, Jeannie. In about a year-and-a-half we were blessed with another gift from heaven, our son Mark. Our toddlers were delightful. Time passed, and You blessed us with two more lovely daughters, Mary Jane and Julie. Life was rich, and we were happy. I thought I would never have to revisit the sadness of our painful miscarriage and the following resentments and misunderstanding.

I was mistaken. Unfinished grieving and glossed-over resentment continued to fester and metastasize, just as cancer spreads throughout the body. At unexpected times, a deep sadness would trouble me, and then I would remember our loss and pain and my loneliness in the grieving. Although I kept my feelings to myself, I often resented my husband's meeting the needs of parishioners, while having limited time and energy for mine.

During counseling with two different counselors, I had sought to deal with the miscarriage. A long time had passed since it had troubled me, and I thought all was well. You knew the extent of the destruction, Lord, and You, as the perfect counselor, knew the timing of complete restoration.

The explosion over the winter retreat was the time. When David came home to a very repentant wife, we set aside ample time for seeking Your help. You had accurately pinpointed the source of my angry explosion as I relived that painful camping memory, although David and I had thought that the miscarriage and following events had surely been dealt with. This time we were ready to let Your Holy Spirit do a complete work.

First we had to deal with our grief and realize that we had not lost just a blob of tissue, but a real person, flesh of our flesh and bone of our bone. At long last we grieved the loss of the baby that we never got to hold, but You graciously revealed to us a fresh hope. We remembered the verses in Psalm 127 which speak of the blessings of children:

> Sons are a heritage from the Lord,
> Children are a reward from him.
> Like arrows in the hands of a warrior
> Are sons born in one's youth.
> Blessed is the man
> Whose quiver is full of them.
>
> Psalm 127:3-5a (NIV)

In addition to our four little ones sleeping peacefully in our home, You helped us realize that we have a fifth one waiting in heaven. Then a new peace came.

But we were not finished. I poured out the pent-up resentment I held against David for being too preoccupied with ministry to meet the needs of our relationship. The root of bitterness had been established at the time of the miscarriage and painful camp experience, but its tendrils had wrapped themselves around other areas of our relationship, suffocating openness and trust and exaggerating little slights. It certainly didn't help that in ministry I often had to play second fiddle to the needs of the congregation.

The original wound of rejection was opened countless times: glaringly so at the time of the arrival of our third child when David was once again ministering at youth camp. Although we had honeymooned on the island just off the coast of our church campground, I no longer had warm feelings for the place. Two times when I desperately needed him, David was committed to ministry there.

Self-pity and resentment are nasty companions. They seem to attract and magnify rejection, even if my dear husband had no control over the circumstances that kept him from meeting my needs. The core of this wound of rejection had been exposed. Now we needed to allow You to lead us through the healing process.

I had tried to forgive David for ignoring me and putting others before me after the miscarriage. I had said the words, but I had somehow held onto the offense. Why couldn't I let go? Then we both remembered the three-step plan of forgiveness from Anne White's ministry.

As we held each other, I relived the pain of that hurtful week and forgave David completely. Then I asked You to no longer allow those offenses to be charged against him, and finally I asked You to forgive me for holding onto those hurts for so long. Suddenly a huge weight lifted, and I was free. Repenting of harboring a grievance was the crucial step to freedom. Counseling with two professionals had not brought the release that repentance plus giving and receiving forgiveness had accomplished.

Yes, Lord, You are the consummate counselor. You know the root cause of every negative, painful emotion and habit pattern. Thank You for allowing the right circumstances for bringing old wounds to the surface, that they might be lanced, drained, and healed.

What a marvelous release and freedom that forgiveness brings. Without my nagging or pouting, David chose to resign from some of his committees so that he could spend more time with the family. You certainly do know how to cause all things to work together for our good.

# CHAPTER 13

# Further Surgery

Thank You for the pain of ruptured "pus pockets" and for the heat of the purging fire. In the summer following my eruption when David left for his winter retreat, I erupted again. This time it happened in front of the children, and I was so ashamed. I had been trying so hard to model godly behavior for them, and now I had just hurled a bucket of sarcasm and pettiness at their father.

After coming home from a quick shopping trip with the whole family, David said to our son, "Mark, get your fishing pole. Let's go down to the pond." Immediately the girls chimed in: "We want to go, too."

"No, girls, not this time. This is a boys' trip," David replied.

Immediately I exploded, saying sarcastically, "Yes, girls, you get to stay home with Mommy and clean the house and wash the dishes. It will be so much fun!"

Another sore had just been exposed. But what was it this time? Later that evening as we sought Your help, You revealed a deep wound that affected my sense of self worth, my view of womanhood, and my attitude toward men in general. All of this affected my attitude toward my own husband and crippled me in our marriage.

I was amazed at how You had orchestrated events leading up to the explosion. A week or so earlier, I had been hanging the white clothes on the line in the bright sunshine. Half-way through the job, I heard a message from You resounding inside of me: "I am going to remove all of the ugly, dark stains from your life."

*That's good*, I thought and continued to hang up the laundry.

Shortly after this experience came the family shopping trip. Herding our little ones through the store, I unexpectedly met an old acquaintance from my childhood—the boy who had lived next door. That "chance" meeting was the kindling wood for the fire to purge me of some serious dysfunction.

Growing up, I had had an on-going love/hate relationship with this young man. Actually, I was jealous of the time he had spent with my dad. Living in the country, I was always excited to get to go to the nearby towns, but all too often I had to stay home with my mother, doing household chores, while the boy next door got to go with my dad. Another source of irritation was not being chosen to help Daddy with some project and having to watch the boy next door being my dad's helper.

As David and I prayed for further revelation, You took me back to my childhood. Painful family conversations played over in my mind. I could hear my aunt relating how much my dad had wanted a boy. When I was born, she had jokingly called me "Henrietta" since I obviously was not a "Henry."

At that moment, I realized that I had lived with the underlying thought that I had been a disappointment to my dad. I had come out of the chute a failure. I couldn't even make it up to him by being a tomboy. Since I was frail and thin, my older sister got to be Daddy's substitute boy by driving the tractor and helping out with the more difficult farm chores.

During all of my life, I must have been trying to make it up to him, trying to gain his approval and validation. That probably had been the motivating factor for striving for perfection in everything that I did. All of the academic honors and 4-H blue ribbons that I diligently earned may have been my attempt to make my dad glad that I was his daughter and to prove to myself that I was worthy of existing.

Although our family did not give any type of rewards for good grades and other types of achievements, I remember my mother's affirmations, but not my dad's.

He was a man of few words. Furthermore, he worked long hours on the farm and at his construction business. Much of the time he was not available, and sometimes he forgot or just couldn't attend important events.

He was a good provider and took an active part in our local church. I was always impressed with his knowledge of the Bible and proud of his church leadership. But I wanted more of his time. I wanted verbal affirmation. I wanted to hear him tell me that he loved me.

I wanted to feel important to him, more important than his work and more important than the boy next door. For some reason, I did not resent my sister's chance to work with him, but I deeply resented someone who wasn't even family getting his time and attention.

The "chance" meeting with my former neighbor had exposed a deep wound and started a series of replays from childhood that underscored the far-reaching effects of not fully experiencing my father's blessing and approval. Continuing to seek Your revelation, I found myself back in the living room dressed as a scarecrow, waiting for my dad to come home from work to take me to the school Halloween party.

As I sat there, I became increasingly uncomfortable as the straw stuffed in my dad's work shirt and farm overalls began to poke and irritate my skin. One hour went by and then another. Sadly and reluctantly, I wriggled out of the costume and dejectedly went to bed. My dad had become involved in a construction project and forgotten about his promise to take me to the party. To him it seemed no big deal, but to a little girl it seemed another instance of not being important enough to be remembered.

Unable to leave this memory, I began to realize that it encapsulated the pain of feeling rejected. Although my dad had been gone for a few years, I sensed that I needed to verbalize my disappointment as if he were sitting across from me. Torrents of repressed hurt and anger and bewilderment began to pour from the depths of my soul. After all of the words came gut-wrenching sobs and then silence.

Graciously You allowed me a physical memory of my dad's presence. A familiar scent of his pipe and a sense of his strong physique surrounded me. I heard myself saying over and over, "I forgive you, Daddy, for forgetting your promise to take me to the party. I forgive you for preferring others over me. I know you didn't mean to slight me. I forgive Aunt Mary for laughingly telling the story of my disappointment to you on the day of my birth. You never told me that you wished I had been a boy.

*But you did choose boys over me, and I forgive you for every time you left me home to do housework, causing me to miss a trip or an adventure. I know you loved me even if you couldn't verbalize it. I forgive you for not telling me that you loved me. I love you, Daddy. I miss you. I wish you could see my babies. I'm glad you approved of my engagement to David. I'm sorry that you were not alive to walk me down the aisle or to see me receive my diplomas. I love you, Daddy. I'm so glad that I will see you again as you welcome me to Heaven.*

Thank you, Lord, for enabling me to pour out my soul and to experience such a vivid memory of my dad. Peace and warmth permeated my being and followed me into another memory. This time I was in my new dorm room saying goodbye to my family at the beginning of my freshman year of college.

My sister and mother had already left the room, but my dad lingered behind. Tears welled up in his eyes and he sobbed while he held me in a long embrace, as if he couldn't bear to leave me. I was stunned, because I had never seen my dad cry, even at his father's funeral.

I also lingered. I lingered in this memory, absorbing its message that I was highly valued and deeply loved by my dad. Then a rush of memories followed: singing with Daddy at the piano, watching the stars with him on a clear summer evening, tromping through the snow trying to follow in his footprints, listening to stories of his childhood. Your blessed gift of forgiveness had restored my trust in my dad's love for me and had assured me that I was worthy of being alive.

When You wash us clean, You know how to deal with every stubborn, crippling stain. Seeing my former neighbor must have been a divine appointment. I had not seen him in over fifteen years. Furthermore, no other person could have elicited such vivid memories just prior to my husband's taking only our son on a fishing trip and leaving the girls at home with mom.

If the healing I had just received in my relationship with my dad had been all that this encounter accomplished, it would have been fruitful enough, but You had much more in mind. Feeling validated by the assurance of my dad's love for me, I was strong enough for further surgery.

The love/hate relationship with my neighbor involved more than just jealousy of the time he received from my dad. As a teenager, he became the handsome school heartthrob. When he walked into the room, you could almost hear a communal female sigh. Although I tried to deny it, he made my heart skip a beat also. And that made me angry.

I did not want to admit that he had power over my emotions. I didn't want him to have any power over me at all. He was my rival, and I wanted to keep distance between us. I tried to be nice and polite, but detached; nevertheless, I couldn't keep my heart from pounding whenever he looked at me with those beautiful brown eyes. I even accepted a few dates with him until he discovered another more attractive interest. I was furious with myself for acting so silly over him, daydreaming about him in class and writing his name on my books.

Now as a grown woman, why was I having such a visceral reaction in this memory? Then You gave me the understanding. Memories of my attraction to this boy brought up the tangled confusion of my own sexual identity.

First of all, I resented men. They seemed to have unfair advantages in our male-dominated rural culture. In my own home, I saw my mother sacrifice her own wants and needs to purchase things for my sister and me, while my father freely spent whatever he wanted on tools and hunting gear. The message to me was clear: men's wants and needs were more important than those of women. After all, they earned the money in most of the homes, and they could dictate how it was spent.

This basic resentment of men's financial power fueled another resentment: men's sexual power. I resented the double standard that seemed to rule in our small community. If a girl told dirty jokes or became sexually active, she was branded with numerous derogatory names and often was shunned; but if a boy bragged about his sexual exploits, he was admired for his sexual prowess by the other guys and excused by the adults with the off-hand comment, "Boys will be boys." I felt

so sorry for the girl who had been taken advantage of
and had to suffer the condemnation of the community.

As a teen, I began to see men as predators that needed to be warded off. In puberty it was easy to get such
a view of males, because nearly every boy that I knew
seemed to have his motor racing. The problem for me
was that the neighbor boy made my motor race, and I
was very conflicted by this. I did not want to admit that
I had romantic feelings and therefore tried to deny and
squelch them.

I determined that I was going to break out of this
cycle of male domination. I was never going to marry. I
was going to pursue a career and be independent. I was
going to be financially and emotionally free. Basically,
I was rebelling against my female identity and denying
my attraction to boys.

One reason for suppressing my feelings was guilt. If
jokes with sexual content were considered "dirty," then
sex itself must be dirty and diligently avoided. Added to
this confusion was the guilt of childhood sexual explo-
ration. What if people knew I had explored my body as
a little girl?

I had once gone through a session of healing of
the memories with my mother's pastor and discreetly
avoided discussing anything sexual. I certainly wasn't
going to share such private information. Later, the enemy had badgered me with accusing thoughts. "What

would the Women's Society at church think of you if they knew what you had done when you were young? You put on such a pious front. You are a hypocrite just like all the others."

One day You broke into my thoughts with Your own thoughts. I distinctly remember hearing You say: "Whatever you refuse to confess will become a tool in the hands of Satan to torment you." This message came just prior to the chance meeting of my neighbor and my angry explosion.

As David waited patiently with me while I processed the torrent of thoughts and emotions, I decided that I needed to confess to my husband every thing that made me feel dirty and guilty. Then I would know for sure that I had no dirty laundry with which Satan could torment me. At first David was reluctant, saying, "I don't need to know everything. It would be sufficient for you to tell the Lord." But I had an urgency to obey the scripture in James 5 that admonishes us to confess our faults to one another that we might be healed.

As I began to release the jumble of fears, confusion, and guilt, I experienced an effervescence of relief and joy. Branding sex outside of marriage as dirty and repressing my own natural sexual impulses made it difficult for me to make the sudden leap of considering sex within marriage as pure and holy and an experience that I could enter into without inhibitions.

Thank You, Lord, for the quick vignette I saw in my mind of a lovely flower-laden bower in the middle of an open field with bright sunlight streaming through. David and I were as Adam and Eve and unashamed within the bower. It was a beautiful and holy place. Through this picture You restored the sanctity of sex in my mind and set me free from years of bondage.

I began to laugh with pure joy. I recalled Your message to me as I was hanging out the white clothes in the bright sunlight. I knew You had fulfilled Your word to me. You had just removed all of the ugly dark stains from my life.

I could reply with great confidence to Satan's accusations of sexual guilt. "You don't have anything on me. I have just confessed everything to my Lord and to my husband. All of my dirty laundry has been washed in the blood of the Lamb and is as white as snow. Look at my clothesline. I have nothing to hide."

When I forgave my father for what I viewed as male chauvinistic attitudes, I began to have a new attitude toward David. Interpreting David's comments and actions through my lens of resentment toward men in general had distorted our relationship. Now we were free to work as a team, each preferring the other in love. Forgiveness had once again brought healing and restoration. Maybe the whole family could go fishing together without the ghosts of the past separating us.

Forgiving my earthly father also freed me to enter into a new relationship with You, my Heavenly Father. I no longer viewed You as too busy to listen to me or too preoccupied with holding the universe together to keep a promise to Your daughter.

Because he was a firm disciplinarian, I had often obeyed my earthly father more out of fear than of love. Without realizing it, I had responded to You in the same way. Filled with a new sense of being loved on a human level, I was released to obey You from a heart of gratitude and love.

Years of purging and deliverance from old wounds continued until forgiveness was becoming a habit. I remember the time when I realized that forgiveness was my first response to any offense. I had been diligently fasting and interceding for a person facing a personal challenge. Not everything was going well, and he had complained to a mutual friend that David was a capable spiritual guide but I could not always be counted on.

For some reason the mutual friend felt duty bound to relay this information to me. For a moment I felt a twinge of pain, but immediately I said inside, "I refuse to receive this arrow of criticism. Lord, You know the hours I have invested in prayer and fasting for this person. I forgive both of these people for negative talk about me. Even if no one knows that I have been the prayer force behind David's counsel, it doesn't matter.

You know my heart. You have seen my tears and heard my prayers, and that is all that matters."

What a victory over possible resentment and self-condemnation! Thank You, Lord, for helping me to forgive immediately instead of taking the comments into my innermost being and feeding on them. Perhaps I was coming closer to that refined silver that reflected the image of Christ. I hoped so.

Little did I know that a more painful challenge lay ahead. Within the church a betrayal by a close friend can seem more difficult to deal with than an attack by a stranger. The cut seems deeper. So it was that Marc Antony said of the wound Julius Caesar received from his dear friend Brutus: "This was the most unkindest cut of all."[4]

I, too, had experienced the pain of a friend's back-stabbing comments and actions. The details of the situation are under the covering of Your forgiving blood, Lord, and I thank You that remind me to let them remain there.

Thanks to the counsel of my mentor, Betty Klem, I had already learned how to deal with the recurring thoughts of painful hurts that seemed to pop up uninvited. I had shared that these thoughts bothered me. I believed I had thoroughly dealt with another wound from a person close to me.

Betty reminded me that once the sins were placed under the Mercy Seat, they were to remain there. To bring them out from under the covering of Your mercy was to give them life and power to bring even more destruction. It has been interesting to hear medical research revealing that reliving a painful experience releases the same toxic chemicals into our bodies as those in the original wounding.

Betty further advised me to quickly offer the pop-up memories to You for Your covering. She also counseled me that once the ax of forgiveness has been laid to the root of bitterness from a long-term unforgiven wound, then lingering memories can be considered little tap roots that work their way to the surface, where they can be extracted and covered with forgiveness.

All of this counsel had prepared me for the challenge of forgiving the person involved in the painful betrayal. But I had to consciously make the choice to forgive daily and to refuse to feed on the hurt.

The ultimate victory in this matter came as I sought You for a message to share at a women's gathering. Isaiah 53 kept coming to my mind. As I read and reread the chapter, the last clause of verse 12 gripped my soul: "For he bore the sin of many, and made intercession for the transgressors" (KJV).

Instantly I knew that You had one more step for me to take. Bearing the pain of betrayal within my being and doing so without complaint, I could continue the forgiving example of the cross by interceding for my betrayer. As I obeyed Your directive, love and compassion flowed freely. I was no longer a victim of betrayal. I was a giver of life and love and freedom. I was learning how to share in the sufferings of Christ and to release His life and His love into a fallen world.

# CHAPTER 14

# Guidance

The process of being conformed to the likeness of Your Son (Romans 8:3) could never have been possible without You diligently training us to hear Your voice and then to obey. Early on, You, Holy Spirit, began by making the Scriptures come alive for us.

Out of desperation we began opening the Bible to seek Your counsel and direction. We would simply open the book, and Scriptures leapt off the page, hitting the problem head on every time. We underlined the passages and began to keep a record of Your speaking to us. For morning devotions I would ask for inspiration, open the Bible, and scan the page for some insight applicable to our lives.

For the first year or so in our new-found partnership with You, our "open and point" system worked very well. Then there was nothing. Search as I would, no verse seemed to speak to me. I wondered if I had somehow lost connection with You. I begged You to restore our system of communication. All to no avail. The Bible well seemed dry.

Praising was not easy either, but I doggedly stayed with my time alone with You. Then one day I received a flash of understanding. It was as if You were saying, "You will no longer treat my Scriptures as a crystal ball. While you were taking your first baby steps, I allowed you to find me in this way. Now it is time to grow up. Immerse yourself in a regular Bible study and listen. I will speak to you in my way and in my time. Keep seeking."

And so I sought to hear Your voice. I was grateful for the times when You sovereignly and without my asking inserted Your thoughts into my mind to guide and counsel me, but there were times that I needed a definite answer to a specific question, and all I found was silence. I desperately wanted to have a dialogue, but I couldn't be sure that the reply was not my own wishful thoughts.

Then someone gave me a wonderful recording. The speaker explained that the "still small voice" sounded just like our own voice in our heads. He instructed us to ask ourselves a question, such as, "Is this Tuesday?" Hearing a simple "yes" was just like the hearing of the still small voice. There had been many times that thoughts sounding very much like my own voice, but with an added dimension, had turned out to be Your guidance.

Sometimes it was hard to tell if the download that I received was actual words or such a thorough understanding that I just thought it was conveyed through words. There were times that You seemed to break into my thoughts with a truth when I wasn't even seeking revelation at that specific moment.

But I also wanted to hear a definite word in response to a direct question. The leader of my Bible study told me, "Joyce, you can receive a 'yes or no' answer from God. Just get quiet. Ask your question. Then listen." Listening was so hard. I would hear "yes," then "no," and then "yes" again. It was so frustrating. I couldn't quiet my own voice. In desperation all I could say was "Help!"

You heard my cry. I was invited to a conference where Joy Dawson was speaking on divine guidance. I drank in all that she had to say and bought her recordings. This gifted teacher taught me to listen and hear and discern. First she explained that there are three voices in the universe: Satan's voice, the human voice, and God's voice. The goal is to silence the first two voices and then trust that the voice remaining is Yours, Lord.

Silencing Satan's voice requires a determination not to be deceived and confidence in knowing one's authority over him through Your victory on the cross. I certainly was determined not to let Satan influence my decisions.

Before I knew that I could confront and defeat Satan in my personal life, however, I had to admit that he exits. Just as Hebrews instructs us that coming to You requires believing that You are (Hebrews 11:6), so it is with our resisting Satan. During childhood, I had no problem believing in his existence as I followed the epic battle between good and evil in the Bible.

I remember following the serialized dramatization of the Bible daily on the radio as a child. I can still hear the pounding of the horses' hooves as the chariots of Egypt pursued the Hebrews to the edge of the Red Sea. I held my breath as You held back the waters, and the last stragglers made it across safely. Then I danced with Miriam as she led the women in celebrating Your victorious rescue.

A chill went up my spine as I listened to the sly lisp of the snake enticing Eve with the deceptive question, "Did God really say that you couldn't eat of that tree?" The same sinister voice made me shudder as Satan asked You, Lord, a similar seductive question, "If you are the Son of God, tell these stones to become bread" (Matthew 4:3, NIV).

In college, the same seducer who tempted Jesus and Eve used the voices of my professors and others in academia to implant a cancerous doubt, "Do you really believe that the Bible is to be taken literally? Do you really believe that Satan is a real entity? You know that the Bible is full of figurative language, especially personification."

As Eve did, I took the bite, and my understanding of Satan as a real enemy faltered. I was an easy target for further deception and unprepared to defend myself. Through events in our son's life, we were about to be blindsided, but You restored our understanding just in the nick of time.

As our radar system sent out signals for Truth, materials came to us from many sources. Some of these materials were too alien for us to accept yet, and so we put them on the shelf in the back of our understanding. Derek Prince's teachings on deliverance from demons very quickly went on that shelf. No doubt You smiled as David and I rolled our eyes at this outlandish teaching series. You knew that one day we would be desperate enough to put it into practice in our very own home.

David was the first one to grab for it the night that our son let out a blood-curdling scream, causing the hair on the back of David's neck to stand up. Rushing back to the bedroom, David found our toddler standing up in his crib, screaming in terror.

Thinking he could quickly calm the situation with a little light, David switched on the dresser lamp. Wide-eyed with fear, Mark stared right past the light at some presence David could not see. When David picked him up, Mark was as rigid as a board and completely unresponsive. No comforting words could reach him. He was deaf to his own father's voice.

Panicked, David reached back for that outlandish teaching. In as forceful a voice as he could muster, he declared, "In the name of Jesus, leave my boy alone." Immediately Mark relaxed and fell peacefully asleep in David's arms.

Somewhat shaken, David returned to the living room to do some serious thinking. When he shared the experience with me, I was relieved that he was the one at home to deal with it. I certainly didn't want to come into contact with something spooky and menacing. I wasn't prepared for such an encounter.

Fortunately, the Bible study I had been attending brought more understanding of the nature of evil and Your provision for combating it. Home alone, I too heard that blood-curdling scream coming from our son's bedroom and forced myself to confront the cause of it. It was a good thing that I had learned about the power of Your blood sacrifice and the power of Your Holy name, Jesus. Calling on that power, I commanded the evil presence to leave.

To our dismay, this was not the last episode. We learned to send that evil force away, but it kept returning. You knew it was time for some drastic action, and mercifully You revealed to my Bible study leader that a young child needed prayer.

When I described Mark's condition, she said that God had shown her a child rigid with fear. Then she addressed the spirit of fear and commanded it to come out in the name of Jesus. For weeks there was no evil disturbance. How thankful we were not to be awakened night after night by this frightening scenario.

The drama was not completely over, though. Mark no longer experienced evil visitations, but he stubbornly resisted falling asleep. The only solution seemed to be to rock him almost endlessly until exhaustion overtook his resistance.

While David was attending a week-long conference, I was being worn down by the draining bedtime routine on top of caring for our three little ones by myself. Sitting in the darkened living room rocking Mark until after midnight, I cried out to You in desperation, "Lord, I can't keep doing this. You'll have to help. I give up."

Suddenly I was blinded by a brilliant light. My first thought was that I must have left the front door unlocked, and I was at the mercy of an invader who was shining a huge flashlight in my eyes.

As I blinked and tried to ward off any attack with my flailing arm, I became aware of a soothing warmth spreading throughout my body, bringing total peace. I felt Mark relax in my arms. Then I knew that You had visited us. How sad I was that I had not recognized that it was You and perhaps could have enjoyed Your presence longer.

Mark was not bothered again until we unknowingly opened a door to allow Satan access to him. On Friday nights, we hosted college students for a fellowship meal. After the kids were put to bed, one young man began to relate his introduction to the paranormal through one of his professors who had taught him to be a medium. Curious, the other students encouraged him to tell them more.

As he began to amaze them with his encounters in the supernatural realm, I heard the unwelcome terrorized scream coming from Mark's bedroom. Rushing to him, I commanded the spirit of fear to leave. Thankfully it did, and soon the students did, too. David and I decided that this particular group would never again meet in our house. I was relieved and thought that we were free from this harassment, but I believe You wanted me to know beyond all doubt that I had power over evil. You are a consummate instructor.

A few weeks later, David was attending an evening meeting, the children were quietly sleeping, and I was relaxing with a good book. My relaxation was rudely interrupted by that same blood-curdling cry. I quickly whisked Mark out to the living room and closed the door to the bedroom wing. I didn't need wide-eyed siblings on the sidelines.

As at other times, Mark was rigid and deaf. He began calling my name, begging me to make "him" stop. I kept assuring him that I was with him, but he continued to call and plead for my help. I waved my hand in front of his eyes, opened wide with terror. He never blinked. He was totally unaware of anything but the tormenting presence. Desperate, I prayed all of the prayers I had been taught. I gave the commands that I have given before, but nothing changed. I needed reinforcement.

Crying out for help, I experienced an overpowering anger that some evil force had entered our home and was tormenting our son. Suddenly I knew who I was in You. I was a representative of the Kingdom of Heaven empowered to defend my home and children against Satan. With a new authority, I commanded that evil presence to leave my son alone, to leave our home, and never to come back. And it obeyed.

Then came understanding. You are real and Your power is real. Satan is real, too, but he is subject to You and to Your followers when we rely on Your conquering provisions made available to us through the cross. I still had a lot to learn, but I was thankful that I had learned that You had indeed given me authority over Satan. Thank You that the evil spirit never returned again.

Silencing the voice of Satan when trying to hear Your voice was not as much of a problem as was silencing other people's voices and, even more difficult, silencing my own voice. I still had to struggle sometimes not to let other people steer me astray, but You were faithful to give me an internal lie detector.

There seems to be a gauge with a very sensitive needle inside of me. When someone is trying to manipulate me or persuade me of some untruth, that needle begins to vibrate, sending out a signal sounding something like, "wonnnnng." Seeking Your truth or direct guidance, I now more forcefully turn a deaf ear to others' voices. The real problem is me. I often want what I want. In other words, I still have a streak of rebellion, at the very least some rather strong preferences.

Surrendering the final say is not always easy. Joy Dawson's suggestion was to determine to put to death my own desires, but that was difficult for me. It was very easy to convince myself that You agreed with me, like thinking You surely were calling us to a marriage ministry weekend in Hawaii in the dead of winter.

Hearing a teaching by Pat Robertson, I began to have a better grasp of dying to self. He taught that we have to come to a place where we have no mind in the matter. If You say, "No," then we also say, "No." If You say, "Yes," then we too say "Yes."

After our move to a new city, You provided a perfect opportunity for me to practice surrendering *my* will to receive *Your* will. Soon after settling into our surroundings in David's new pastoral appointment, I received a call from the president of the local Women's Aglow Fellowship. She said she felt impressed that You had chosen me to take her place as president.

Right away I knew that her hearing must have become a little dull. You had never mentioned that matter to me. And I had no intention of doing any such thing. I marshaled all of my arguments to convince her that I could not possibly comply.

Although I had just resigned as president of the Aglow chapter in our former city, I did not believe You were calling me to this assignment. I already had enough on my plate. Our children needed my time and support in adjusting to a new church and new schools. I needed to give my husband extra support in his new assignment, and I needed time and energy to adjust myself.

Besides, the policy of Women's Aglow dictates that the full board appoints the new president after much prayer. The custom has always been to choose someone who has been trained within the local group, not a total stranger. I had visited the chapter only once, and the board had no way of really knowing me, except that I had been their speaker during that one visit.

REAL FAITH IN THE REAL GOD IN THE REAL WORLD

Furthermore, and finally, I knew that You would not want me to accept. In my mind the matter was settled, but not so in hers. She asked me to ask You about the matter and said she would get back to me. Since she was not planning to resign for a few months, I had ample time to seek Your will.

The first thing I did was to remind You of all of the reasons I could not possibly take on another responsibility, just in case You might not have been aware of my situation. How noble of me! Then I sought counsel from those sympathetic to my point of view. Of course, I had first informed them of my already busy schedule. They quickly concurred with me. *Good,* I thought. *That settles that.*

All too soon the Aglow president called back and did not accept my refusal. "I really sense that God is calling you to this job. Would you please pray again? I'll get back to you." I was frustrated. I thought I had settled the question, but what if You really were asking me to take this job?

Reluctantly I agreed to pray. As I thought about it, I realized that I had not been seeking Your will but informing You of what I thought Your will was. I had not been listening because I was too busy talking. I decided to put the steps to hearing Your voice into practice.

First, I commanded Satan to be silent, reminding him that You had given me authority over him. Then I began trying to silence the human voice. I asked You to completely put to death my old tendency to try to please people and determined that I would follow no one's voice but Yours.

Next I had to deal with my voice. I remembered the teaching on having no mind in the matter. Cautiously I ventured, "If You say, 'No,' then I'll say 'No.'" That was easy. "If You say, 'Yes...'" I could not bring myself to agree with a "yes" answer. In frustration, I gave up.

Being the good teacher that You are, You did not. At 3:00 a.m., I was suddenly awake thinking about having to give my final decision. Tossing and turning, I became very agitated. "I might as well go pray. I'm not getting any sleep anyway," I muttered to myself.

Sitting alone in the dark living room, I began my listening routine, but I couldn't get any further than I had during the day. I still could not agree with the "yes" answer. Trying to come to a place of "having no mind in the matter" was more difficult than I thought it would be. On this matter I certainly did have a mind of my own.

Night after night I went through this struggle. Then I remembered teachings on peace. One pastor friend had shared that when he had to make a choice between two conflicting options, he simply chose one and then waited to see if he had peace about the decision.

That corresponded with others' references to Paul's instructions in Colossians 3:15 (NIV): "Let the peace of Christ rule in your hearts...." I certainly needed an arbiter, an umpire, to settle this internal battle. Hanging onto my stubborn refusal to give up my will was making me miserable. I was becoming irritable from lack of sleep, and I had no peace at all. I determined that I had to surrender my stubborn resistance.

That night at 3:00 a.m. I once more returned to the dark living room, but this time I threw myself on the floor more out of desperation than surrender. Then I began the routine. Once again I still paused at completing the "yes" step. For a long time I lay face down in the avocado shag carpet, trying to surrender.

At last I pummeled the carpet with my fists and sputtered: "Okay, I'll do it!" To my amazement, I was flooded with peace. Going back to bed, I slept like a baby. I had finally silenced my own voice. The ensuing months confirmed that a "yes" answer was indeed Your will for me, because I received so much understanding and experience in walking in Your presence through that particular job.

Bob Mumford had already taught us that circumstances are part of confirming Your will. Thank You for sending us teaching at just the right time. Mumford shared that when a ship's captain positions his vessel so that the harbor lights line up in an exact row, he knows he is on target for a safe entry. Correspondingly, we can be sure that we are entering Your harbor, Your ordained will, when we see the three harbor lights of an inner witness, Scripture, and circumstances coming into alignment.

You must have enjoyed our first venture in checking the validity of this teaching. I had heard about the gathering of Christians in Washington D.C. to pray for the nation. Immediately I had "an inner witness" that our family should be included. David was less than enthusiastic. He dislikes long bus rides and big crowds, and this trip involved both. But the major obstacle was the money to cover all six of us. We didn't have it. "Please pray about it, honey," I begged.

How could a pastor refuse that request? Settling into his prayer chair, David began a time of worship, meditation, and listening. After a while he came into the kitchen wearing a wry smile. "Guess what scripture popped into my mind? 'I will give you thanks in the great assembly; among throngs of people I will praise you'" (Psalm 35:18, NIV).

Yay! We had two of the harbor lights: an inner witness and a confirming scripture. Of course, without a specific scripture, we knew that my longing to go was not in conflict with Your written will. Your Word is replete with admonishments to pray, including encouragements to pray for those in authority.

The last harbor light would require a definite change in our financial circumstance. David and I agreed that whatever extra money came our way would go for the trip. David says he thought he was safe because he didn't anticipate any opportunities for more money coming our way, but You had a plan. Throughout the next week, You began sending money from unexpected sources until every member of the family was covered, except one.

David gallantly volunteered to stay home. How shocked we were when our dear friend Doris Downey stopped by the house to say that she felt You had impressed her to pay for one of our children. In a few short days, You had supplied the exact amount needed for all six in our family. And we had all three harbor lights: inner witness, Scripture, and confirming circumstances. Discovering Your will was becoming a fun adventure.

Thank You for tuning our ears to hear Your voice and for opening our eyes to see Your plan. We no longer had to wander about in confusion and futility. You were giving us Your heavenly GPS. I loved explaining Your guidance to teenage campers in terms of a maze. Like rats in a laboratory maze, we often find ourselves bumping into dead ends and scurrying about trying to find the right path. How reassuring to connect with an all-seeing, all-knowing loving Father, who from the vantage point of heaven, can direct our steps.

# CHAPTER 15

# You Speak

How thankful I am that I made a connection with You as a teenager. Although I was not very adept in always following You, You knew how to get through to me. You knew how to send me a message and to set up roadblocks to prevent me from going down a path that You had not ordained.

I think again about hearing your voice about my future mate. Believing You had sent me my life partner, I was so shocked to hear a message contradicting that conclusion. Looking across the room at the young man I was dating, I clearly heard, "He will not be the father of your children." I had not heard Your direct voice since the time You spoke to me to dedicate my life completely to You.

I was taken off guard, and I suppressed that message. I didn't want to believe that I was really hearing from You, but circumstances proved that You had a different plan for both of us. The more I tried to hold onto that relationship, the more it disintegrated. Thank You for putting up roadblocks to redirect us both toward Your better plan for each of us.

Years later, I was no longer trying to block out Your message. With the husband You had ordained for me, I was desperately seeking Your guidance, and You were richly rewarding our search.

Once we had begun actively seeking Your presence and Your direction in our lives, we found that You were everywhere attempting to speak to us. You spoke to us through nature, through other people (even our kids), through Scripture and other literature, through music, through circumstances, through a quiet understanding, and through Your still small voice.

Someone has said that You are continually broadcasting to the human race; the problem involves our receivers that need to be tuned into the right station. Thank You for confirming that understanding with the verses in Isaiah 50:4-5 (KJV) "the Lord God... wakeneth morning by morning, he wakeneth mine ear to hear as the learned."

When we were trying to tune our ears to receive Your direction in changing churches, You didn't let us down. Because this was the first time making a move since the children were enrolled in school, we wanted to make sure that we did not miss Your will.

In the weeks before visiting the new church, we kept seeking guidance. We knew You had made it clear that we were to move, but the new destination was unclear. All the way to the possible new church we kept saying, "We are going to listen with everything within us. We are going to hear God's voice."

You have such a sense of humor, Lord. No doubt You had everything orchestrated, even down to the choice of bulletins. David and I could not keep from laughing when we were handed a bulletin, on the cover of which was the picture of a large ear with the scripture: "He that hath ears to hear, let him hear" (Matthew ll:15, KJV).

Every hymn, every congregational reading, and every Scripture lesson pointed to taking this assignment. When we were reading aloud the passage from Isaiah, I began to giggle. I could no longer deny that You were speaking clearly to us.

I hadn't wanted to move, citing how good it was to be in our present location. But You spoke pointedly to me through that Scripture reading: "Forget the former things; do not dwell on the past. See, I am doing a new thing! Now it springs up; do you not perceive it?"(Isaiah 43:18-19, NIV). Underneath my breath, I kept saying, "I get it. I get it."

When I was going through a period of doubt and fretting over a delayed answer to prayer, You lovingly pointed me to the visible proof of Your bounteous character revealed in nature.

I will never forget the understanding and peace that came to me when I heard the message in my spirit: "When you come to me wringing your hands in fear and unbelief, you offend My magnanimous character. Look at my creation. Look at the infinite varieties in every species. I am lavish in my creation, and I long to lavish my love upon you. Don't come crawling to me, begging and fearful. Come running to me as a child expecting wonderful gifts from a doting father." Now as I look at the blaze of fall colors or the myriad of spring flowers, I hear the resounding message that You lavishly love me.

Receiving from nature is sometimes easier than receiving Your message through human beings, but You proved that You can speak clearly through other people—even our children. I surely was surprised one morning when I was grumpily fixing breakfast after a difficult night with little ones.

From out of the blue our little two-year old preached me a salient sermon from her high chair: "Bring some joy, Mommy. Bring some joy." I looked up immediately to acknowledge the source.

Sometimes it is hard to acknowledge You as the source because You pick unlikely messengers, like a speaker that I often disagreed with and so did not readily value his instruction. He often ridiculed my enthusiasm for the work of the Holy Spirit. I was sure he was not as spiritual as I.

You knew how to deal with that pride. On Saturday evening, 2 Chronicles 35 popped into my head. Checking it out, I was disturbed by the story of the righteous King Josiah who refused to believe that You could use the Egyptian King Necho to speak to him and as a result lost his life. I remember saying, "There surely is some vitally important message that I must not miss. I wonder who my Necho is?"

The next morning I was a little irritated to find my least favorite speaker was giving the message. I was even more irritated to read that his topic was on religious fanaticism. "Humpf! The nerve of this guy." I was about to tune him out when I heard him say that the problem he had with overly zealous Christians is that they get so excited with the froth and excitement of spiritual experiences that they fail to move on to maturity.

That struck a nerve inside of me, and I realized that You wanted me to get that message. I do have a tendency to revel in the excitement and bubble over telling everyone all about what You have done for me. There is a reason to "ponder all these things" in the heart. This allows a time of deep feeding and of communing with You. In sharing prematurely, the energy is expended, and I have little left to let the revelation or experience transform me or to offer back in appreciation to You. I had just encountered "my Necho."

Thank You for not only speaking through unexpected sources, but also through even off-hand comments. When You sensitize my antennae, my spirit can pull in messages that otherwise would have gone right past me, just like the one when we were listening to classical music with some friends.

We were all absorbed in the rich, full swell of the complete orchestra, when someone said, "Isn't it amazing to think that all of those individual parts were once in the mind of the composer as he wove them into one beautiful composition?"

"Beep, Beep, Beep." In that instant You were beaming into my receiver the answer to a long-time question from childhood. "How can You hear my prayers above the cacophony of voices from all over the world in thousands of languages and dialects?" The answer was immediately clear. In Your infinite mind You can hear my little piccolo in the midst of blaring trumpets and booming basses.

Music seems to be a favorite vehicle of communication for You. Sometimes my thoughts consume me as I wrestle with problems, but You very easily by-pass that mental traffic jam by starting a tune subtly playing over and over until I am forced to acknowledge it. Then the words begin to penetrate my thoughts, offering me a solution.

I vividly remember Your intervention during one of my worry sessions when the economy had taken a nose-dive. All across the nation, people were scrambling to find creative ways to help the family budget. It was February and time to begin preparing for next year's garden by ordering seeds and starting the seedlings under grow lights.

We were blessed to live on a little thirteen-acre place with some of the richest soil David had ever had the pleasure of gardening. He used to jokingly say that when he planted seeds in that wonderful sandy loam soil, he would have to jump back to avoid trampling the plants springing up.

What a disappointment when for the first time in our gardening experience the Burpee Seed Catalogue refused our order because of a shortage. One evening after I had put the children to bed and had finally gotten around to finishing cleaning the kitchen, my mind was filled with questions of how we were going to feed our four little ones on a limited budget.

I was thinking, "We certainly will have to can and freeze more fruits and vegetables and probably invest in some locally grown chickens and beef for the freezer. But where are we going to get seeds for the garden?

We surely had made a mistake by using only hybrid seeds. If we had used the straight-line variety, we could have saved the seeds and not been without this year. I wish we knew some Amish families well. Maybe we can make some contacts to purchase straight-line seeds and not be without for next year and the year after that."

Throughout this monologue a tune was playing in my head. When I finally stopped to listen, I began to sing the words, "Oh, yes, I'm feasting on the manna from a bountiful supply for I am dwelling in Beulah Land."

I began laughing and repenting and thanking You at the same time. "Oh, Lord, You heard my fretting. Please forgive me for trying to solve problems on my own. You are our provider and You will take care of us. Thank You for reminding me." Sure enough. You provided seeds and the garden grew. How thankful I am for that reminder of Your faithfulness in song. Time and time again You have gently instructed me with music.

Sometimes Your instruction has not always felt gentle but lovingly firm and consistent. In the midst of training me to hear Your voice, You have been training me to obey. I think "Obedience" has been a lifetime course for me. When we were very young, my sister and I were asked to sing a duet in church. We practiced over and over until the lyrics were deeply ingrained within me: "Trust and obey, for there's no other way to be happy in Jesus, but to trust and obey."

Years later, You brought another song on obedience that still sings inside of me. Mysteriously a copy of a choral number appeared on our piano. It wasn't something that the choir was currently practicing, and no one in the family knew where it had come from. Maybe it was a stray piece of music that had been picked up with other copies we had borrowed from the church, but the message certainly wasn't an accident.

As I skimmed through the pages, my attention was riveted on the refrain: "Obedience is better than sacrifice. He is much more interested in our listening to Him. More than offerings, He wants us to know Him." Thank You, Lord, for teaching me that knowing You in intimate fellowship can happen only through listening and obeying.

I remember being captured by Your solemn pronouncement in Deuteronomy that in order to remain under Your umbrella of favor and blessing, the Israelites needed to "hearken diligently" to Your voice and "to observe and to do" all of Your commandments (Deuteronomy 28:1, KJV).

When I read "hearken diligently," I felt that as a loving parent You had taken my face in Your hands and said, "Are you listening? Do you hear what I am telling you? Take My words seriously and always obey them." I had read the results of the Israelite's not listening and obeying, and I wanted to avoid repeating their mistakes and reaping the same disasters.

Even though I would wonder at their foolishly turning away, reaping a punishment, crying out for Your help, receiving restoration, and then walking away from You again, I knew that I had the same tendency. I wanted to be like Moses and Joshua and wondered why it was that they could remain obedient when practically everyone else fell away.

The answer came in a recorded message from Bible teacher Ern Baxter, who pointed out that Moses and Joshua spent much time in Your presence and heard Your voice first-hand. Although Joshua did not get to accompany Moses into Your presence on the mountain, he did follow Moses into the "tent of meeting" outside the camp, and after You had spoken to Moses and Moses had returned to the camp, Joshua lingered in the tent (Deuteronomy 33).

Because of their fear, the people withdrew from Your presence. When You manifested Your presence on Mt. Sinai, they said to Moses, "Speak to us yourself and we will listen. But do not have God speak to us or we will die" (Exodus 20:l9, NIV). They did not realize that they had chosen to cut themselves off from the source of strength to obey.

Later when I was absorbing Andrew Murray's teaching on obedience, I was thrilled to hear him confirm the same message. "It is the joy of ever hearing the Father's voice that will give the joy and strength of true obedience. It is the voice [that] gives power to obey the word; the Word without the living voice does not avail."[5]

Although You had allowed me to sit under many gifted teachers of Your Word, I knew that I had to seek Your guidance and understanding for myself also. I had to go up the mountain through praise and worship daily to receive Your direct impartation of truth. You alone knew the exact path that I was to follow. Isaiah 50:4-5 (KJV) summed up what You had been teaching me:

> The Lord God hath given me the tongue of the learned, that I should know how to speak a word in season to him that is weary; he wakeneth morning by morning, he wakeneth mine ear to hear as the learned. The Lord God hath opened mine ear, and I was not rebellious, neither turned away back.

At last I was entering into dialogue with my creator, just as had David Wilkerson, the author and pastor who had inspired my original searching. Your words were so life-changing that I didn't want to lose any of them.

I had studied some teachings on journaling, but the instructions seemed too complicated for my busy lifestyle. I didn't have time to categorize my entries. I believe You helped me settle on a simple but effective pattern of recording the scripture, song, or thought and then asking for Your application for my life.

When I received that application, I wrote it down and asked You to work it out in my life. My Bible study in conjunction with praise and worship was not very scholarly, but it surely was practical. You began to work Your will and purposes into the fabric of my life as Your applied Word shaped my thought and actions. When I came across Andrew Murray's comment that "Scripture was not given to increase our knowledge but to guide our conduct."[6] I knew that I was experiencing that process firsthand.

# CHAPTER 16

# My Faithful
# Parenting Guide

Seeking and obeying Your Word was not a heavy burden but an exciting adventure with the best teacher humanity has ever known. Your instruction on parenting was the best example of Your efficient and thorough teaching skills that I can remember.

While You were teaching us how to instill obedience in our children, You were putting us through our own boot camp of obedience. Sometimes I felt as if I were in the hands of a relentless drill sergeant; at other times I knew that I was being supported by a gentle encourager. Through it all You sprinkled in enough laughter to help us revel in our new-found skills and discipleship fitness.

It all started with two scriptures. During morning devotions verse 7 of Proverbs 20 caught my attention: "The just man walketh in his integrity; his children are blessed after him" (KJV). Immediately I was convicted of my sloppy parenting practices and of slipping back into negative attitudes and impatient comments. I moaned, "O, Lord, I'm not walking in integrity in our home and our children are not going to be blessed in the future because of my example."

Taking my red pen, I underlined the passage liberally. Then, seeing that the red ink had bled through the page, I turned to see what else I had inadvertently marked. How You must have laughed at my consternation! Your Word had nailed me again. Verse 18 of chapter 19 in Proverbs hit me right between the eyes. There were Your Words glaring at me through the red ink and commanding me to "Chasten thy son while there is hope, and let not thy soul spare for his crying" (KJV).

"You mean 'spank him?' I can't do that. I've determined to reason with my children and not to resort to corporal punishment."

But You and I both knew that wasn't working. I was trying to follow the latest psychological philosophies because I wanted to be an enlightened parent. Seeing my confusion, my mother had advised, "Throw out Dr. Spock and his ilk and use your own common sense."

In my confusion, I tried both approaches, thoroughly confusing the children. One day I was consistently strict, making them follow my correction. On other days after I had failed miserably at reasoning, I threw up my hands, thinking, "Oh, do what you want. Just don't burn the house down."

They never knew which Mommy they were dealing with until they had misbehaved royally. Needless to say, the children were embarrassingly unruly at times. Sometimes I despondently pondered their future and nervously envisioned them in some juvenile center for the incorrigible. They needed a consistent, godly administration of correction, and I needed to understand my parental authority in Your plan for family life.

I had carefully noted Your initial instructions, but I was having trouble following through. I was still trying the reasoning approach and attempting to force myself to stay calm in the face of open defiance. I just couldn't spank. I didn't want to hurt their little psyches.

Our evening bedtime routine was a circus. Lining up four little ones in the bathroom, I issued four tiny toothbrushes. Administering the proper amount of toothpaste on the brushes of the two older ones, I nudged the smaller ones to the second sink to do the brushing myself.

Invariably little hands surreptitiously snatched the toothpaste tube to create interesting designs on the counter. Calmly I would say, "Don't squeeze the toothpaste." Turning to the little ones, I could glimpse another blob of the white goo oozing out onto the counter. More forcefully I would issue the command: "Don't squeeze the toothpaste!"

With each repeated infraction the volume was rising, and so was my blood pressure, until I would rage with my blood vessels bulging: "I said, 'Don't squeeze the toothpaste!'" By that time I had forgotten all about my qualms over spanking and felt like pulverizing the little beasts. I didn't, but I feared I had already left welts on the inside by my tongue-lashing.

In contrition I would kneel by the bedside to repent and beg Your help. You must have decided that I was an experiential learner and sent some old friends to demonstrate proper discipline. Our seminary friends Dave and Ann came with their son, Brent, who was just about our little ones' age.

During the course of their visit, I observed their method of discipline and noted that Brent was calm, confident, and usually instantly obedient. When he dallied too long after a command, Mom or Dad would count to three. If he failed to comply by the third count, his parents would remind him of their command and then administer a swat to the backside, followed by a reminder to start earlier next time. Our children resisted correction, whined, and whimpered. Clearly our friends were using a superior method.

In the weeks that followed their visit, I experimented with commands, counting, and correction. My problem was my reluctance to bring swift punishment. I wanted to give them ample opportunity to comply; therefore, I counted "1, 2, 2 1/2, 2 ¾, 3-3-3-3-3-3." I still fell back on trying to reason and then resorted to shouting. I needed more help understanding discipline and my place of authority.

After sending a live demonstration, You followed with a scriptural explanation of discipline. The next issue of one of my Christian magazines featured an article entitled "Children: Fun or Frenzy?" by Pat Fabrizio, later published as a pamphlet *Under Loving Command*. I could easily identify with the "frenzy."

"Chaos" was another word for the confusion in our house in the area of discipline. I was still struggling with the resistance to spanking and therefore, I was inconsistent and uncertain, even a bit fearful, when confronted with disobedience.

All of our children were willful, but our first-born was definitely the epitome of the strong-willed child. Although I had not yet read Dr. James Dobson's classic book on the subject, I was living its content. Jeannie was sweet and creative, but she was also determined. Added to this determination was a very logical mind and superb language skills. After her skillful defense of her actions, I was almost nodding my head in full agreement. David and I decided that she was destined for a brilliant career as a lawyer.

But there was another entity in our little courtroom, the Supreme Judge, who had written the law for all humanity, including a reluctant, spineless mother. As a mostly compliant child, I was buffaloed by the strength of the self-will in our children. In my own weakness, I delayed enforcing the law, actually a simple spoken command, until I had reached the point of exasperated explosion.

Regrettably, I was destroying their self worth and respect more than if I had applied a corrective switch without the raging anger. I was also creating an atmosphere of hostility, resentment, and regret. I needed correction as much as the children, and I heartily agreed with Mrs. Fabrizio's assessment of the situation: "Anger and hostility toward the child is the result of our own disobedience as parents to not chasten as God commanded us, or from our delay in obeying until we become frustrated."[7]

Lord, I was convinced that I needed to diligently study and implement Your plan for bringing up children. How thankful I was for this concise defense for godly discipline, complete with convincing scriptures. The discussion that training was more thorough and lasting than merely teaching intrigued me. I had often heard the Proverbs 22:6 (KJV) injunction to "Train up a child in the way he should go; And when he is old he will not depart from it." Mrs. Fabrizio's discussion of this wisdom made it very clear. The dictionary gives the meaning of the word train: "to mold the character, instruct by exercise, drill, to make obedient to orders, to put or point in an exact direction, to prepare for a contest." This is what God wants us to do with our children. The child who is only taught "the way he should go" can hear other teaching and depart. But the promise to the parent who trains his child is, "When he is old, he will not depart from it."[8]

We wholeheartedly endorse training as necessary in all endeavors, especially athletics or artistic performance. The groaning of athletes after a hard workout suggests a sense of punishment, not pleasure. The serious fitness enthusiast submits to grueling workouts by a personal trainer. Often, I have merely studied and been taught the importance of proper diet and exercise, but without painful application, I have always failed.

In the discipline of our children, I was determined not to fail. I wanted our children to look back and say, "Thanks, Mom, for making us obey." I wanted to be a good coach, a trainer according to Scripture. I desperately wanted to be a faithful "doer" of this Word.

I desired that You affirm my faithfulness as You described Abraham's faithfulness. "For I know [Abraham], that he will command his children and his household after him and they shall keep the way of the Lord, to do justice and judgment: that the Lord may bring upon

Abraham that which he hath spoken of him" (Genesis 18:19, KJV).

You had spoken a promise to me in my anguish over my poor parenting skills. I cried out for help and You whispered "Isaiah 54" in my mind. The whole chapter spoke of Your kindness and restoration to a broken people, but verse 13 spoke Your promise to me as a beleaguered mother: "And all thy children shall be taught of the Lord; and great shall be the peace of thy children" (KJV).

I had been relieved to think that You would do the teaching, but now I began to think that You might be accomplishing that task through my training. And what about the differentiation between "teaching" and "training?" Thank You for my Hebrew scholar husband who clarified my confusion. Looking up the passage in the original language, he found that the Hebrew word for "taught" is "lamad," which carries the connotation of "to goad, the rod being an oriental incentive."

The Hebrew clarification brought me back to my quandary over spanking. The use of "the rod" in Scriptures on discipline left little doubt as to Your chosen method, but "rod" brought up images of metal bars. Surely You were not advocating cruelty. Again my scholar husband helped me to understand that "rod" comes from the word for "branch" with the meaning of a stick for punishing or walking.

My mother had "lovingly" used the yardstick on my plump place to correct my disobedience. Until I learned to use the stick as a mom, I didn't understand the import of her oft-repeated statement: "I'm spanking you because I love you." I remember telling the children that if I didn't love them I would not bother correcting them, because it took a lot of time and energy.

It would have been easier to ignore their foolish choices, but I loved them too much for that. *Children—Fun or Frenzy* made it clear that You intended the stick to be used as an instrument of loving correction. "He that spares the rod hates his son; but he that loves him is diligent to discipline him" (Proverbs 13:24, KJV).

It was Pat Fabrizio's description of disciplining her children with the rod or stick that helped make the application of the Scriptures understandable. Motivated by a desire to obey Your teachings and to love her children with a commitment for their good and not her convenience, she diligently and calmly used the switch every time they failed to obey.

My obedience to God to train my child requires that every time I ask him to do something...I must see that he obeys. When I have said it once in a normal tone, if he does not obey immediately, I must take up the switch and spank him (love demands this) enough to hurt so he will not want it repeated.[9]

Because she used the switch consistently and without anger or rejection, her children became secure and experienced peace. After each correction, she took time to hug and to remind them that she was obeying You by insisting that they learn to obey.

Her ultimate goal was that her children would be prepared to walk in obedience to You for a lifetime. "If we are faithful to train the child to bring his will into submission to ours, I believe (and have seen) the child will transfer that submission to God as he grows older. But if he takes our word lightly, he will take His word lightly."[10]

Encouraged, I decided to face the challenge of explaining the new rules to the children and to follow through on any needed correction. You must have anticipated my possible weakness, because I believe You arranged for the final motivation for diligence.

Out of the blue, my cousin from a neighboring state called to say that she and her family would like to come for a weekend visit. We had not spent a weekend together since we were teenagers. Because we were close in age and used to have a grand time together, I eagerly made the necessary plans.

Little did I know the plans that You had for me. After the first day of our visit, I became aware of the differences between our two sets of children. Our four were boisterous and slow to obey. Linda's five were calm and instantly obedient. I watched with interest as she told her youngest to eat all of her vegetables. Without protest or dalliance, she complied.

That evening after the children were all sleeping peacefully, Linda and I reminisced over old times, especially our family gatherings at our grandfather's farm. After laughing at our hilariously good times, Linda became pensive.

"Not all of my memories are pleasant ones," she said. "I was aware of how the rest of the family viewed my sister and me. I know the names they called us. I know they used to say, 'Watch out! The wild ones are coming.' We were very undisciplined. You and Jane were the angels. Isn't it interesting how our children turned out?"

"Ouch!" my insides cried. "Okay, Lord, You just got my full attention. Daily determined discipline has just begun, with a large dose of Holy Spirit assistance, of course, please."

The teaching part of the regimen went well; it was the follow through that was a little shaky. I just didn't have a good sense of my own authority. I felt weak inside administering the corrective switch, actually a wooden paint stick. As the consummate instructor, You sent the final installment of the months-long curriculum: Laddie, a rambunctious ball of fur.

One problem with our new pet was that he didn't stay a cute, cuddly little puppy. All too soon he grew into a large unruly pest. David's mother would call before coming to visit to make sure the monster was restrained. For some reason, she didn't appreciate muddy paws on her shoulders and sloppy kisses on her cheek.

Laddie, a mixed breed of German Shepherd and Husky, was very friendly, as well as very rowdy. I don't really remember wanting Laddie, but the children did, and I believe You did, also. When it was time for dog obedience training, David did the primary training in the class, but we both decided that I needed to be able to control him also.

After a few classes, David decided that the classes were mainly to train the owner as well as the dog. As I began participating in the training, I knew that that was definitely true. I had to learn to exercise authority over this brute, and that was no easy lesson.

I had to first realize that I had authority. Then I had to overcome my fear of crossing his will. He did not want to heel, and he definitely did not want to sit. One evening while struggling to force him to heel, I realized that he was clever, almost human. Just like the children who were resisting obeying, Laddie began to play.

Jumping and licking my face, he seemed to say, "Don't you think I'm cute? Come on, let's play."

Knowing that You were expecting me to learn an important lesson by exerting my authority, I gave a quick jerk with all of my might on the choker collar. Normally my pulling on the collar had little effect because his Husky neck was so thick.

This time You must have given me an assist because Laddie stopped playing abruptly. Slowly and deliberately, he placed his huge jaws around my wrist and looked me straight in the eye. For a moment it was a stare down. Then I blinked. I wish I had called on You for help. Instead, I cried, "Daviiiiddd!" Fortunately for me, David heard me through the kitchen screen door and came to my rescue.

After a few brisk walks under David's grip, Laddie was docile enough to submit to my control. Thank You for helping me to face my fear and take the leash once more. I felt like a person thrown from a horse and having to get right back in the saddle. Of course I felt more secure with David nearby. Laddie had already submitted to his authority, and I was praying he would recognize my authority soon.

Choosing not to walk away in defeat caused me to realize that I did have authority, and that must have been the turning point for Laddie also, because he never resisted me again.

Walking him without David at home was a bit intimidating at first, but praying calmed my nervous jitters. My relationship with Laddie was clearly a clash of wills that I had to face and to win. I had to continue the daily training to be sure Laddie knew who was in charge.

I needed to know that I was in charge of not only Laddie, but of our children, also. Sometimes their defiance was very intimidating, and I felt like shrinking back from confrontation. Summoning my determination and seeking Your strength, I began to face each challenge with swift correction.

David and I decided that every prospective parent should have to take a dog through obedience training well in advance of the arrival of human "puppies." The instruction we received was life-changing for us as parents.

We had to give vocal commands, show the dog exactly what that meant, and make him comply immediately. We were not allowed the luxury of giving up by saying, "Well, he doesn't want to cooperate right now. We'll try again tomorrow."

No, we had to stick with the training until the dog obeyed as soon as we gave the voice command. Disobedience to the voice command had to be met with a quick jerk on the choker collar to train him that failure to comply meant pain. This was repeated until the choker collar was no longer needed. The ultimate victory came when not even the leash was necessary. Hour after hour we repeated the exercises in heeling, sitting, staying, and coming.

At the same time we were training our little Julie to stay seated in her high chair. All too soon little ones learn the art of unhooking restraints, which she would accomplish quickly and then stand teetering back and forth, smiling as if to say, "Aren't I cute and clever?"

Dutifully trained himself, David began the arduous task of applying Laddie's training to his little girl. He would give the voice command, pull back his chair, walk to the high chair, repeat the command, and make her sit. By the time he had reached his own chair, Julie would have popped back up with the same playful smile.

Time after time, day after day, Daddy repeated the same process. Then came the day when all he had to do was give the command and pull back his chair, and Julie sat down. Finally the ultimate obedience was accomplished. Daddy gave the command and Julie sat down. I think we all cheered. In prayer time we thanked You that one day our children would hear their Heavenly Father's voice and instantly obey.

When I look back on those months of training us to discipline our children according to Your Scriptural instructions, Lord, I am amazed at Your diligence and thoroughness. You knew that I desperately wanted to be like Abraham, who commanded his household to keep the way of the Lord so that You could fulfill Your promise to bless him and make him a blessing. I clung to Your promise in Isaiah 54:13-14 that all of our children would be taught by You and that they would experience peace.

You did not disappoint me. First You gave me Your instruction in the Scriptures; then You brought two live demonstrations of obedience training in action. To make sure I understood Your complete plan, You brought Pat Fabrizio's thorough discussion of Biblical discipline, and then You sent Laddie.

When our daily regimen with Laddie had shown us how to exercise authority, then peace began to reign in our home. The children became calmer and more confident because they knew what was expected of them. They also knew that You were holding us accountable just as we were holding them accountable. Clearly the good work You had begun, You carefully carried on to completion, just as You promised in Philippians 1:6.

# CHAPTER 17

# God Woos Our Children

Just as we had been training our children to listen to our voices, we knew that Your higher purpose was for them to recognize and obey Your voice through a love relationship with You. One by one, they asked for help in inviting You into their hearts. The fact that they came without our prompting was amazing to us. Through this we witnessed the validation of Jesus' declaration: "No one can come to me unless the Father who sent me draws him" (John 6:43, NIV).

Their salvation experiences came without any emotional hype or coercing. In the course of playing, bathing, and looking at nature, they made their simple requests. One evening while dancing about the house with her siblings, our six-year-old Jeannie, who had already prayed the salvation prayer with us, announced that she wanted to be filled with the Holy Spirit. No doubt she had heard us discussing our encounter with Your Spirit and was eager to have the experience also. After reading the Scriptures in Acts, she simply asked and received.

While I was pondering how much she really understood, Jeannie ran back to her bedroom and returned with her most valued and jealously guarded treasures and began to distribute them to her three siblings. I was dumbfounded! She would never even let them touch her valuables. Now she was giving them away. Clearly I was witnessing a miracle.

But the more profound expression of that miracle came in the following days and years. From that time on, our strong-willed, argumentative child became an eager-to- please, obedient wonder. When she was a teenager, she was appalled when classmates would tell their parents that they were going one place and then sneak off to a forbidden place. She said she could not conceive of hurting us by lying. She still had strong opinions, but after her encounter with Your Spirit, she was never again defiant.

Our son, Mark, was alert to all the wonders of nature. In the spring he delighted in discovering each new budding flower and in exploring nests in the trees he loved to climb. He was also an early riser. Life was too exciting to miss by snoozing till 6:00 a.m. or 7:00 a.m. Awake at 5:00 a.m., he first wanted a hearty breakfast and then he wanted to check out the world. After convincing him that it was too early to play outside, I would often sit with him at the large living room window.

On a branch just outside the window, we watched a mother robin build her nest and then tend her eggs. Mark was thrilled to observe the little blue shells on the ground and discover the nestlings extending their beaks for an early breakfast.

One morning while watching this little drama, Mark said that he wanted to ask You into his heart. He couldn't wait for the rest of the family. He had to do it right then. After listening to the scriptural plan of salvation, our little five-year-old bowed his head and invited You to come into his life. It was a quiet beginning, but the commitment was powerful enough to take him through many tough times in the years to come.

Mary Jane is our intuitive, creative child. Interrupting her play one day, she climbed into my lap and asked me a very profound question, "Mommy, when did you first know Jesus?" I answered, "Well, my mother read the Bible to me and I studied about Jesus in Sunday School."

"That's not what I mean, Mommy. I don't want to know when you first learned about Jesus. I want to know when you first knew Jesus." I was speechless for a moment. Was this our little four-year-old speaking or was this a learned theologian pinpointing the essence of Christianity? Surely there must be an inner longing for You, God, within all of us—even in little four-year olds.

When I regained my composure, I told her of Your wooing me as a little girl and my simple response of asking You to forgive my sin and to come into my heart. Her immediate reply was "That's what I want." I tried to convince her to wait until Daddy came home, but she was insistent on immediate action. When I had read the scriptural basis for repentance and receiving, Mary Jane repeated a simple prayer and then hopped down to continue playing.

She had responded to Your call and was ready to go on with life. Years later she would be leading other little children in similar prayers through Child Evangelism, Project Evangelism in Ireland, and an outreach to inner-city children in the States.

Over the years, I have marveled at the ease of our children responding to Your claim on their lives in very natural, everyday settings. One evening while in the bathtub, our little Julie, only three years old, announced that she wanted to ask Jesus into her heart.

Again, this request came as a shock. I hadn't made any suggestions that she needed to do this. We hadn't even been discussing anything spiritual. Was getting clean physically a prophetic act of getting clean spiritually?

At first I hesitated to follow through on her request. How could someone so young possibly grasp the import of salvation and a lifetime of relating to her creator? Just as her sister had been, Julie was insistent. Thank You for helping me to explain the Scriptures in simple language. Without hesitation she simply asked You to come into her heart.

Months went by and I hadn't thought much about that evening. I assumed that Julie would have forgotten it and would come to You when she was more mature. I guess I was the one with limited understanding of Your dealings with little ones. The next summer I was surprised to find that You had indeed made a more lasting impression on our little one that I had imagined.

At the dinner table, the children were asking about being ready if the second coming of Christ should happen in their lifetime. They were wondering if they would somehow miss hearing the call to follow You. I assured them that they had each established a relationship with You and would be able to hear whatever You might have to say to them.

One of them immediately expressed concern over Julie, saying, "But Julie won't know. She's never asked Jesus into her heart." Sitting up very straight on her chair, Julie announced confidently, "I have too. I asked Jesus to come into my heart in the bathtub." No doubt You were thinking, "Oh, ye of little faith."

I had not even celebrated Julie's new life with the rest of the family, but I am sure the angels were rejoicing around Your throne when she bowed her head in the bathtub and became a part of Your eternal family. Now as I observe the spiritual strength she exhibits in rearing her own little brood, I celebrate bathtub conversions.

# CHAPTER 18

# Faithful Counsel

Your diligence in fulfilling Your promise to nurture our children has always amazed me. You are a faithful God. You spoke Isaiah 54:13 to my spirit, promising to teach our children Yourself and You painstakingly executed that plan.

Thankfully You implemented that plan clear through puberty to adulthood. When struggling with the exhausting early years, I remember older mothers admonishing me to cherish those times. "If you think you are busy now, just wait until the teen years," they told me. I couldn't grasp how I could be any more stretched than I was already, but when I found myself trying to cope with the hectic schedules of four teen and preteen kids into sports and music and clubs, I understood.

What a blessing that You didn't leave us during those tumultuous years. When our last child turned 21, David and I exchanged "high-fives" for surviving puberty four times. But You are the One who deserves the credit. We made plenty of mistakes, which You redeemed, and You intervened countless times before a major blunder.

When one of our daughters withdrew from us during junior high school, I cried out to You for a way to re-establish communication while still respecting her need for privacy. During prayer time a solution popped into my head. Why not try writing a daily letter similar to the love letters we had experienced in the marriage seminars we led?

Every letter started with an affirmation of something we appreciated in our spouse, setting the tone for positive communication. Then we explored the feelings we experienced in relation to the topic of the letter. We never accused or blamed. We spoke only about our own thoughts and feelings in an effort to let our spouse enter into our world.

Explaining the plan in a spiral notebook, I left it on her bed with the understanding that only if she chose she could respond and leave the notebook on my bed. Without any pressure she responded. Slowly, but surely, she came out of her shell and we could share freely again. Thank you. You helped me avoid the mistake of nagging, finding fault, and snarling communication lines.

I had made that mistake a few years earlier with her brother. I became irritated when older girls began calling him at the end of sixth grade in school. Calling boys was a "no-no" when I was growing up. Their persistent pursuit of my son made me angry. I didn't handle the situation well. My irritation began to spill out in my interaction with my son.

After hearing them gush about how he "looked just like Shaun Cassidy," a teenage heartthrob at the time, I noticed that he was beginning to comb his hair to look like their hero. That really unsettled me, and I mistakenly began to remind him to be himself and not let others define who he was.

Lecturing definitely wasn't the answer. It only led to defensiveness and differences that seemed to escalate into a very strained relationship until his comments over lunch one day exposed a deep rift. By this time he was in junior high and had come home alone for lunch. Looking across the table at me, he said, "Mom, why do you hate me?"

"Oh, honey, I don't hate you. I love you."

"No," he said. "Every time you look at me, you disapprove." With that, he excused himself and headed back to school.

I was devastated. How had I failed my son? I loved him so much, but I had wounded him. I had created a hostile environment, and we were wary of each other. In desperation I cried out to You and You heard my cry. In a few weeks after that lunch encounter, I attended the International Conference of Women's Aglow Fellowship in Chicago, where several hundred women from around the world had gathered.

Following the crowd into the huge ballroom on that first evening, I sat down at the nearest available table and found myself seated directly across from a dear friend I had not seen since moving many miles from my husband's last church appointment. And right there You had an appointment for me! In that sea of women only You could have arranged our meeting.

When she inquired how life was going for me and my family, I burst into tears. "Oh, Patty, I am losing our son. Everything I say comes out wrong. He takes offense so easily, and I get defensive myself. We just can't communicate. He's only in junior high. What will it be like when he's in high school and we have really serious issues?"

Then I told her the whole scenario of girls' flattery, his choosing to look like Shaun Cassidy, and my nagging him to be himself. She said, "Joyce, I completely understand. We are just coming out of a similar situation with our son Jimmy. He went off to college a clean-cut, responsible kid and came home scraggly and unkempt with long, greasy hair, and he brought home some of the most bedraggled friends. Our trying to fix him in our image only made him surly and resistant.

I didn't know where to turn, so I turned to God. After much prayer I believe He gave the answer. I clearly heard in my head, *Look for the good and ignore what you consider the bad, for what you speak to is what will come forth.* We've been following these instructions, and our communication with Jimmy has been renewed. Amazingly, he is beginning to discover on his own who he is and where he wants to go and how he intends to get there. And it is all good."

Then she added, "Joyce, don't worry about your son's following a role model. We all need someone to look up to. One day he'll find the right role model, and will pattern his life after Him."

I returned home with hope and a plan. Early in their childhood we had established a pattern of sharing and praying with each child separately at bedtime. Throughout the day I began thinking about and looking for the good I saw in Mark.

At first I began rather woodenly telling him that he was such a good boy. Soon the more I looked for the good, the more I saw. I would rub his back as I shared my appreciation. I began to realize that he was no longer just tolerating my touch, but relaxing and receiving my thoughts as well. I was no longer nagging or lecturing because there was little to complain about. Finally we could look into each other's eyes in peace and trust. You had saved us. And I am so grateful.

I didn't think much about my friend's comments about emulating a role model until Mark's senior year in high school. One day I had invited a member of our church to have dinner with us. I was preparing the meal while she sat at the kitchen table and shared some of her loneliness and discouragement.

In the middle of our conversation, Mark burst through the back door. Usually he quickly breezed through the kitchen in a rush to the shower after his grueling cross-country practice. But when he saw our guest, he stopped to sit down beside her, engaging her in conversation. When he finally did excuse himself and head for the shower, Joy said, "You don't know how much that meant to me. Usually teenagers never notice me, let alone take the time to actually talk with me. I feel so much better."

Later that evening when I stopped by his bedroom to rub his back and chat, I told him how much his reaching out had meant to her. He turned over and said, "Do you know why I did that, Mom? That's what Jesus would do, and I want to be just like Jesus." I smiled and said an evening prayer with him.

When I returned to the kitchen, I paused to ponder our conversation. Then loud and clear I heard Patty's voice: "Someday he will find the right role model." Tears rolled down my cheeks as I bowed my head and thanked You for Your faithfulness.

As I look back over his life, I realize that You diligently provided excellent role models wherever David's ministry took us. As a counselor's kid at our high school church camp, he learned that zealous Christians could also be "cool." During the afternoon sporting events, many of the guys dazzled the crowd with their athletic prowess and in the evening devotions they unashamedly shared their faith, even weeping openly when they talked of Your redeeming their mistakes. There he learned that "real men" love Jesus.

I will always be grateful that those young men included our son, who was much younger than they, in their inner circle and thus validated him as a man. Many of them kept in touch with him during the year—a real investment for busy teenagers. As a teenager himself at the same camp, he developed lifetime friendships that continue to nourish him and his walk with You. As a little boy he wanted a brother. He got three sisters, whose influence made him a very caring, sensitive person, and in time You provided the brothers he needed.

He really needed a big brother when we moved from our rural community to a more metropolitan one. There he encountered bullies. As a slender-built kid, this must have been intimidating, although he never complained about it. He had left many close friends at his former school. I remember praying for Your intervention, that he would not become bitter at You because of Your call for us to move. Being a preacher's kid had enough challenges.

Once again You provided a big brother—two, in fact—twins in our church, who were top scholars and athletes. Both spent time with him. After one of them had given a weight lifting demonstration for Mark's scout troop, he invited him to join him in lifting weights twice a week. What a gift: companionship and muscles. Through all of Your dealings and the relationships you provided You raised our son up to be a Christ-like role model himself.

# CHAPTER 19

# Conclusion

Now with children grown and gone, I sit in the quiet house and contemplate Your faithfulness. You never failed me. You claimed me when I was a child; You called me in my teen years; You corralled me when I was about to stray from Your choice of a life mate; You kept me in college; You rescued me from depression and healed me in the inner depths of my soul. Then You guided me through the many pitfalls of parenting.

But the best gift of all was Your revelation of Yourself. You became my Savior, rescuing me from a life of self absorption and rebellion against my creator. How tragic it would have been to live disconnected from the source of all power and creativity and miss Your destiny for my life. Although I wandered and I strayed many times, You saved me over and over, always forgiving and restoring.

When I nearly drowned in remorse and self hatred for failing a loved one and thrashed about in waves of regret, continual self-accusation, and apologizing to You over and over, You lifted me with one question. "Who is your Father?" Suddenly I saw myself, the prodigal, standing before the outstretched arms of the welcoming Father. My blubbering apologies ceased, and I fell into Your embrace restored.

Faithful, Omnipotent, Omnipresent, Omniscient loving Father, Savior, Counselor, You have proved yourself over and over in my life. You are not a fairy tale character or a wish fulfillment of a needy people. You are life. You are love. You are truth. You are the source of all that is. You speak. You inspire. You teach and guide. You love. You sacrifice Yourself for us. You forgive. You restore. You call us into covenant relationship. And You never forget us. You never stop reaching for us. We are engraved on the palm of Your hand.

In my spiritual confusion and times of depression You kept me from drowning in my doubts and fears. You threw me Your lifeline of hope through Scripture, accounts of changed lives, and Your still, small voice. In the vortex of swirling needs and responsibilities, You steadied me with wise counsel and supportive mentors.

In my new freedom You taught me to sing and soar with You, to laugh and celebrate with You, and best of all, to dance with You. You truly are the lover of my soul. You pursued me with relentless love. You are real and You instilled real faith in my soul in this complex real world.

# Endnotes

1. Emily Dickinson, "There Is No Frigate Like a Book," *Poetry for Kids: Emily Dickinson*, ed. Susan Snively (Bend, Oregon: Moon Dance Press, 2016), 3.

2. E. Stanley Jones, *Victory Through Surrender* (Nashville: Abington Press, 1966), 13.

3. Jones, *Victory*, 14.

4. William Shakespear, *Julius Caesar*, (3.2.188).

5. Andrew Murray, *The School of Obedience* (Radford, VA: Wilder Publications, 2008), 24.

6. Murray, Obedience, 25.

7. Pat Fabrizio, *Under Loving Command*, (Cupertino: DIME Publishers, 1969), 12.

8. Fabrizio, *Loving Command*, 8.

9. Fabrizio, *Loving Command*, 10.

10. Fabrizio, *Loving Command*, 16-17.

# Bibliography

Dickinson, Emily. "There Is No Frigate Like a Book." In *Poetry for Kids: Emily Dickinson*, 3. Edited by Susan Snively. Bend, Oregon: Moon Dance Press, 2016.

Fabrizio, Pat. *Under Loving Command*. Cupertino: DIME Publishers, 1969.

Jones, E. Stanley. *Victory Through Surrender*. Nashville: Abington Press, 1966.

Murray, Andrew. *The School of Obedience*. Radford, VA: Wilder Publications, 2008.

Shakespeare, William. *Julius Ceasar*. (3.2.188).

CPSIA information can be obtained
at www.ICGtesting.com
Printed in the USA
JSRC030917020521
14119JS00002B/1